Financial Planning

for

Poor People

Financial Professionals Guide to Working with Low-Income to Middle-Income Individuals

by

Dr. James M. Moten Jr., MSFP, CFP®, ChFC®, AFC®, CMFC®, CRPC®

Dr. C.W. Copeland, ChFC®, CLU®, RICP®

Dr. Kimberly Turner, MSFS, CFP®, ChFC®, CLU®, CAP®

Table of Contents Page

Introduction

Why are we writing this book? Because there is a need to help those with little wealth to acquire more wealth by using sound financial knowledge. Just like you, we too, have experienced sometime during our life feeling broke, busted, and /or disgusted. However, we have managed to rebound to a higher financial ground.

This book is intended for those who do not make a lot of money but want to financially secure their future. We know that you will make mistakes along the way, but it is how you recover from those mistakes that matters. This book aims to share sound financial principles; so, that you know what "right" looks like. Our hope is that after reading this book, you will be empowered to make the best financial choices given your situation. More importantly, this book will arm you with the skills that you will need to help to decide when is the correct time to act "pull the trigger" and get on track.

About the authors

C. W. Copeland, Ph.D.

C. W. Copeland, Ph.D. is the President of the Financial Planning Division of the National Financial Group. Dr. Copeland is also an Adjunct Professor of Insurance at **The American College of Financial Services,** an Adjunct Professor at the **College for Financial Planning** and an Adjunct Professor at **Clark-Atlanta University**. Dr. Copeland conducts scholarly research in Behavioral Economics and teaches graduate-level business courses. He has been a regular guest on radio and television shows across the country where he addresses audiences on financial planning strategies on a regular basis.

Dr. Copeland has served for 22 years as an instructor with R.S. Thomas Training Associates providing pre-licensing training, continuing education, and business development advice for financial services professionals. Dr. Copeland has more than 20 years of industry experience as a financial planner where he coordinates the efforts of attorneys, tax advisors, employee benefits coordinators, estate and business planners, and pension managers for the benefit of his clients. He holds numerous licenses and registrations (in multiple states) in the areas of investments and insurance and holds the prestigious Chartered Financial Consultant (ChFC®) and Chartered Life Underwriter (CLU) designations.

Kimberly Turner, Ph.D., MSFS, CFP®, ChFC®, CLU®, CAP®

Her interest in retirement planning was piqued at a very young age. It stemmed from her passion to help families to develop financial freedom and financial security during retirement. Her goal is to help at least one family a day to create the retirement lifestyle of their dream!

Kimberly is the Founder and President of Prosperity Doctors LLC dba The Retirement Planning Doctors.

She is currently the Vice President of the Financial Planning Division of the National Financial Group. Also, she is an adjunct professor at California Lutheran University where she teaches graduate level courses in financial planning, investment planning, insurance/ risk management, and retirement income planning.

She obtained a dual in Ph.D. in Financial Planning and Retirement Planning from the American College of Financial Services in 2019. Her dissertation focus was on creating a bridge between health planning and financial planning. She obtained her master's degree in Financial Services from the American College of Financial Services 2012.

She entered the financial industry in 1998 **as a real estate developer. Then subsequently, she became the** broker/owner of a top producing multi-office real estate company that received numerous awards. During this time, she became the owner/managing partner of a real estate title company and a mortgage company. After the great recession, she transitioned into the capital market and risk management sectors in 2009 to help clients build more diverse wealth portfolios.

Prior to becoming a real estate developer/real estate broker, her interest in healthcare and affordable medicine led her to pursue studies in Health and Science at the University of Florida. After completing her studies to become a physician assistant, she practiced within the field of internal medicine.

She holds numerous licenses and registrations in the areas of real estate, mortgages, investments and insurance and holds financial industry renown designations, Certified Financial Planner (CFP®), Chartered Financial Consultant (ChFC®), Chartered Life Underwriter (CLU®) and Chartered Advisor in Philanthropy(CAP®).

James M. Moten Jr., PhD, MSFP, CFP®, ChFC®, AFC®, CRPC®, CMFC®

Dr. James M. Moten Jr., is the Program Director and Assistant Professor for the Masters of Science of Financial Planning Program at The American College of Financial Services. Additionally, he is the Vice President of the Financial Planning Division of the National Financial Group. He is a former Personal Financial Counselor for Zeiders Enterprises and Advisor and Registered Representative for Primerica Finance Services.

Dr. Moten has a PhD in Business Administration (Financial Management Concentration), a Master of Science in Finance, a Master of Science in Accounting, a Master of Science Economics, a Master of Business Administration, a Master of Science in Financial Planning and a Master of Science in Acquisition and Contract Management. In addition to his academic degree's, he holds the Series 7, Series 6, Series 65, Series 63, Series 26, Life and Health, and Property and Casualty Licenses in multiple states. Lastly, he holds the Certified Financial Planner CFP®, Chartered Financial Consultant ChFC®, Accredited Financial Counselor AFC®, Chartered Mutual Fund Counselor CMFC®, and Chartered Retirement Planning Counselor CRPC® professional designations.

Dr. Moten has published three textbooks: *Advanced Financial Management: Theory and Application*; *Introductory Financial Management: Theory and Application*; and *Personal Financial Literacy: A Practical Approach* through BVT Publishing. Dr. Moten also co-wrote "Chapter 17: Insurance and Risk Management" for Victor Ricciardi's book *Financial Behavior: Players, Services, Products, and Markets*, published by Oxford Press.

ISBN: 978-1-7368119-0-0

Published: March 4, 2021

Chapter 1

Financial Literacy

Financial Literacy

Financial literacy is centered upon having the appropriate education, the skillsets, and the understanding of how to make optimal financial decisions. Having the ability to utilize various financial tools in order to maximize financial gains and minimize financial losses is powerful. Knowing how to create and protect wealth is a key element to having to financial success. Having the ability to make informed financial decisions to create wealth builds confidence. Confidence strengthens one's ability to take appropriate actions as needed without lingering. Financial literacy influences how one applies knowledge to best generate, invest, spend, save and protect wealth. This concept is applicable to both individuals, organizations as well as institutions. Individuals must be able to balance a checkbook, comprehend personal income taxes, understand the concept of the compounding of interest, as well as understand the importance of a proper budget in order to make wise decisions about money. These skills are vitally important; nonetheless, many individuals are without this basic financial knowledge and therefore are experiencing lack luster results with their finances. Business owners, on the other hand, must have an understanding profit and loss statements, risk analysis, production schedules, marketing operations, and many other types of financial reports in order to make the best decisions the future of the company.

Financial Capability

Financial capability is an essential ingredient of financial savviness. Without it, clients may remain stagnant and fail to take advantage of valuable financial resources or be harmed by misusing them. The financial industry as well as the overall economy benefits from financially capable households who actively and responsibly use financial services. Our goal is to empower households to take advantage of the positive waves of financial offerings and to steer clear of less optimal financial offerings that they are likely to encounter during their lifetime. Financial capability is not just having financial literacy skills, but also having the eagerness, the confidence, and the resolve to proactively move towards making the best financial decision at a point in time wher meeting a specific economic challenge.

Albeit, financial knowledge acquisition, financial information, and financial skills development play a vital role in developing the financial capacity of a person, they do not totally explain the strength of intentior or the motivation necessary that causes one to act, or the potential barriers which causes one to remain inactive. Psycho-social influencers may overcome barriers or obstacles to active money management There are primarily two psycho-social theories that broadly defines financial capability, **attitude** and **self-efficacy.** A person's positive or negative behavioral actions towards the importance of managing finances is *attitudinal* and their belief or confidence in their ability to achieve financial goals is *self-efficacy*.

Our definition of financial capability also includes management decisions that are best suited to the circumstances in which a person lives. In other words, a person's lifestyle and culture influences how the make financial decisions. The phrase "decisions that best fit the **circumstances** of one's life" reflects the fact that people in different ag cohorts, communities, aspirations, and health statuses, are met with a variety of economic challenges. One person's solution for a specific challenge may be very different, however, equally fitting, than another person's decision given the same situation. They may both exhibit financial capabilities, yet it is expressed in different ways. For example, a 40- year old who was recently diagnosed with a chronic illness may elect to liquidate their retirement account and incur the 10% penalty for an early disposition of funds because of their need to cover the gap for their household expenses that emerged due to lower earned income levels. Their decision to incur the 10% penalty was influenced by the reduction of earned income because of their illness as well as limited additional resources. On the other hand, another 40-year-old may decid to acquire a home equity line of credit to help fund the gap of their household expenses which occurs as a consequence of lower-than-expected earned income levels.

Lastly, financial capability maybe encouraged by economies of scale for **enabling environments.** Enabling environments include financial markets, social, political and religious structures in which one resides. It is important to realize that certain enabling environments have a greater influence than others and they have a greater impact on one's financial capability. For instance, individuals who hold religious institutions in a higher esteem when compared to the government, would display a greater tendency to seek out and follow financial guidance from a religious entity. Also enabling environments may offer different incentives to promote positive financial behaviors (i.e., tax cuts and personal recognition. Furthermore, a person's intention or motivation to act is influenced by how he/she thinks other experts, family and friends, expect them to respond to an economic challenge.

In conclusion, we define a financially capable person as someone who:

1. Understands the importance of managing money proactively (attitude)
2. Stands willing to implement appropriate financial decisions without hesitation
3. Has the necessary skills to take advantage of newly acquired financial knowledge
4. Is confident that she or he can act on that desire (self-efficacy)
5. Has access to an environment that empowers them to place their desires into motion

Self-Efficacy

A person's confidence about his or her ability and capacity to achieve goals or to deal with the challenges of life.

The Role of Self-Efficacy

Most people can set goals they desire to accomplish, list things they would like to modify, and cease doing things that are harmful. However, most people also realize that setting plans into action to accomplish specific goals is worrisome and not quite so simple. Bandura and others have noted that an individual's level of self-efficacy influences how they approach goal attainment, carrying out tasks, and overcoming challenges.

People with a weak sense of self-efficacy:

- Stay within their comfort zone
- Shy away from difficult tasks
- Believe that they are incapable of overcoming challenges and difficult situations
- Are overly sensitive about the possibilities of personal failings and negative outcomes
- Quickly lose confidence in personal abilities to resolve issues appropriately

People with a strong sense of self-efficacy:

- Are keenly focused and have deeper insight into the activities they participate
- Welcome new challenges and views them as opportunities to shine
- View difficult problems as tasks to be learned and mastered
- Have greater passion and a higher commitment level towards their interests and activities
- Bounce back faster from disappointments and setbacks

Sources of Self-Efficacy

How does self-efficacy develop? Self-efficacy starts to develop in early childhood as children deal with a wide variety of circumstances, experiences, teachings, tasks, and conditions. Furthermore, self-efficacy continues to emerge throughout one's life span as people encounter new situations and experiences, acquire new skills, and develop higher levels of understanding.

There are four major sources of self-efficacy:

1. Psychological Responses

Our personal responses (rational reactions and emotional reactions) to situations play a vital role in the development of self-efficacy. Moods, emotional states, physical reactions, and stress levels may affect how a person feels about their personal beliefs as well as their ability to perform in a particular situation. For example, a person who has a tendency to become anxious before speaking in public may develop a weak sense of self-efficacy in a similar situation.

Albeit, Bandura in his article notes "it is not the sheer intensity of emotional and physical reactions that is important but rather how they are perceived and interpreted." When one learns how to control their personal responses to a particular situation this will enhance their self-efficacy. By learning how to acclimatize to stress and negativity when presented with difficulties or burdensome tasks, people can raise the level of their sense of self-efficacy.

2. Mastery Experiences

"The most effective way of developing a strong sense of efficacy is through mastery experiences," Bandura explained. Performing a task repeatedly and successfully improves our sense of self-efficacy. On the other hand, when one fails to adequately deal with a task or challenge this may undermine and cripple self-efficacy.

3. Social Persuasion

Bandura also highlights that people may be induced to believe that they have the skillsets, capabilities, and resources to succeed. For example, when someone receives a compliment, positive reinforcement, or encouragement they are more likely to achieve their goals. Both verbal and non-verbal encouragement helps people to overcome self-doubt and feelings of inadequacy as well as realigning their best effort to accomplish the task at hand.

4. Social Modeling

As people see others accomplishing similar goals which they set for themselves this gives them hope. Also, witnessing others successfully completing difficult tasks nourishes self-efficacy. According to Bandura, "Seeing people akin to oneself succeed by perseverance raises the observers' beliefs that they also possess the power and capabilities to master similar skills to succeed."

Locus of Control

There is a theory in the psychological literature known as *locus of control* that is unknow to most people, even though, once it is defined, is widely understood. Locus of control is an individual's belief system regarding the causes of his or her experiences and the factors to which that person attributes success or failure.

The Locus of control concept is generally divided into two camps: external and internal. When a person has an external locus of control, and they expect they will succeed they are highly motivated and more likely to learn compared to if they expect to fail. A person with an external locus of control, who attributes his or her success to luck, happenstance, or fate, will be less likely to make the effort needed to learn and move ahead. People with an external locus of control are also more likely to experience anxiety and fear since they believe that they are not in control of their personal lives. On the other hand, when a person has an internal locus of control, they attribute their success to their` own efforts and abilities and they are quite motivated to learn new things to move ahead. They experience less anxiety because of their confidence, and they feel in control of their personal lives.

This is not to say, however, that an external locus of control is "bad" and an internal locus of control is "good." There are other variables to be considered, nonetheless, psychological research has found that people with a more internal locus of control seem to have better opportunities during life, e.g., they tend to be more goal oriented, plan setters, achievers, and earn higher salaries.

I had the opportunity to teach real estate professionals for years. Each Realtor was interested in learning how to develop a stream of clients that they could serve within their practice. Some, who had experience, took the course because they were not doing well and wanted to learn how to become more successful. During the introductory remarks by each student, I was able to mentally divide the class into those having an internal or external locus of control and, therefore, learn a great deal about the class composition. The "externals" would say things like, "no one wants to buy real estate, the market is slow, "it's too hard to succeed these days," or "the competition in our field is killing me," etc. The internals clearly believed and accepted that it was, essentially, up to them to succeed. The externals believed that luck, fate, or circumstance would more likely determine whether or not they would or would not become successful, more than their own skills, education, strength and motivation.

On the contrary, the "internals" would say things like, "If it is to be, it is up to me, I must train to become successful," "What can I learn to become more successful," "I am responsible for what happens in my practice," etc. (Notice the context of each statement).

Locus of control is often viewed as an innate personality component. However, there is also research that notes it is modified by childhood experiences—including children's interactions with their friends and family members, especially their parents. Individuals who were encouraged to be independent thinkers during their childhood are more likely to understand that there is a connection between actions and consequences. Independent thinkers tend to have an internal locus of control versus an external locus of control.

There is research that supports the premise that children who were raised with an internal locus of control have more successful outcomes as adults compared to those with an external locus of control. One stud looked at the potential health effects of the locus of control trait. This study evaluated more than 7,500 British adults who were followed since birth that showed an internal locus of control by the age of ten. This study revealed that individuals that displayed an internal locus of contro as children were less likely to describe their health as poor, were less likely to be overweight at age thirty, and less likely to show high levels o psychological stress as adults. These findings suggest that children with more internal locus of control tend to exhibit healthier behaviors as adults because they have higher levels of confidence in their ability to affect outcomes through their own actions. In addition, they may have a higher level of self-esteem.

Behavioral Finance

Individuals that invest capital to generate more capital are called investors. According to traditional finance or economic models, individuals should behave in a rational and logical manner. Investors are typically identified as having one of three different types of attitudes for risk (risk adverse, risk neutral, and risk tolerant). Most investors are *risk averse*, which means that when they are faced with two investment options that have a similar expected return but different risks, the investor will select the one with the lower inherent *risk*. Risk adverse investors usually invest their money in certificate of deposits, government sponsored entities, market mutual funds or whole life insurance. Similarly, investors with a neutral risk attitude often select lower risk investments. However, *risk neutral investors* are indifferent to the level of risk and are mainly focused on their desired rate of return. On the other hand, investors who are *risk tolerant* are on the opposite end of the spectrum. They are risk takers. Risk tolerant investors select investments with a higher level of risk, for an opportunity to earn highe profits. In general, risk adverse investors seek to avoid risk. Risk toleran investors look to invest in volatile investments, and they are willing to accept the associated inherent risk. The risk neutral investors fall with-ir the middle of the two extremes.

These three risk attitudes attempt to illustrate the way rational investors respond to risky situations. However, behavioral finance attempts to explain how investors are irrational and their responses to a given financial situation is not just based on their own perception of risk alone; but, their own biases as well. Behavioral finance suggests that market participants make irrational systematic errors that are contrary to the way rational markets participants should behave. Some divide behavioral finance theory into three sub-categories: biases, heuristics, and framing (Shefrin 2007).

Biases

A *bias* is a tendency to lean towards a particular way of thinking that can lead to bad judgment and/or irrational decision-making. Biases can stem from cognitive, psychological, personal preferences, social economics, and cultural influences.

For example, a cultural influence may hinder an individual's financial decision to purchasing high risk investments. Most African Americans steer away from equities because they are raised to believe that slow and steady is the best way to build wealth; so, the selection of equities is less desirable. The stock market is associated with volatility and non-guaranteed rates of returns. Also, Hispanics (59%) are less likely to purchase life insurance than blacks (66%) and whites (62%), (LIMRA, 2013). Many Hispanics (75%) believe the cost of insurance is too high and 49% remain uneducated about what type and which policy to buy (LIMRA, 2013). As a result, when Hispanics are considering purchasing life insurance, they are slow to purchase.

Heuristics

Behavioral finance recognizes that biases and heuristics, such as anchoring, the framing effect, and mental short cuts, influence the judgment of people, causing them to carryout actions that are contrary to their desired results. Moreover, as people develop various behavioral heuristics, they become more confident and subsequently more susceptible to irrational financial decision making (Cox, 2015). In short, a heuristic is a shortcut that people use to solve a problem when they are overwhelmed or too lazy to put in the effort to solve it the proper way.

Although a *heuristic* is a general rule of thumb or a mental shortcut that helps people to increase the speed of their decision-making ability it can lead to suboptimal results. These shortcuts present a problem when they hinder one's ability to develop new ideas, digest new information, or when someone faces anomalous circumstances.

The following biases are examples of heuristics, including availability, representativeness, and anchoring.

The availability heuristic is when you make a judgment about something based on how *available* examples are in your mind. For example, if you were visiting a new city and all you saw were older people you would be led to think that the city's population was skewed towards senior citizens.

While the availability heuristic has more to do with one's memory of specific instances, the representativeness heuristic has to do with one's memory of a stereotype. For example, short people are better at playing the guard position than the forward position on a basketball team.

Anchoring is a heuristic that people use when they are trying to make a decision starting from an anchor or focal point as a reference or starting point. For instance, when people rely too heavily on the very first piece of information they learn, this may have a serious impact on the decision they end up making.

The *framing effect* is a heuristic that is an example of cognitive bias in which people respond to a particular choice in different ways depending on how the choices are presented. If the choices are framed as a loss or framed as a gain, people tend to select the option that was presented in a positive frame.

Heuristics influences people to make snap decisions based on their gut instincts that lead to less than favorable outcomes.

LESSON#1: BASICS

Financial Basics are just that - *basics*. But keep in mind that although many of your clients will have a *basic* understanding of these concepts, there is a high probability that they are not actually putting their knowledge into practice. An important part of your role as an advisor is to be able to not only explain key concepts but also to help your prospects and clients understand WHY it's so important to their financial future to APPLY the basics in their everyday life.

In this section, we are going to cover 5 key topics that are simple, but critical to helping your clients achieve long-term financial security: Income vs. Net Worth, Liquidity, Interest, Budgeting, and Insured Limits on Investments.

LIQUIDITY

Liquidity can be thought of as the ability to quickly convert an asset to cash, with limited or no lose in value. Businesses, unlike individuals, use liquidity ratios (i.e. Current Assets divided by Current Liabilities) to evaluate their ability to meet cash obligations in the near future. However, it is important for individuals to maintain a high-level of liquidity unless they have a guaranteed stable income or reliable access to short-term credit.

How do you define liquidity? Would you say that it is the same definition that your client's use? Access to cash has been the typical solution for the liquidity problem; however, since cash has some minor limitations (i.e. chance of being lost or stolen), it is important to consider appropriate substitutes that will enable your client to function as if they had cash in hand. Such substitutes would be checking/savings accounts, money market deposit accounts, short-term certificates of deposit, money market mutual funds, cash values from life insurance, and Treasury Bills.

Why is liquidity important in your client's portfolio? Without liquidity, your client's portfolio, and possibly their financial stability, is at risk. The best investment strategy in the world is foiled if no money is available for an emergency when it occurs. Consequently, emergencies, and likewise liquidity, must be considered as part of your client's overall financial plan.

When would a Liquidity Ratio be relevant to your client? One scenario would be when they are applying for a mortgage. The lender would look at your client's debt-to-income ratio where they would add up all of your client's debt divided by their gross monthly income. A borrower with a high debt-to-income ratio is more likely to run into trouble making their loan payments.

<u>FDIC & SIPC</u>

The Federal Deposit Insurance Corporation (FDIC) was developed to insure the deposits of investors in case of bank failure. Likewise, the Securities Investors Protection Corporation (SIPC) was developed to insure the deposits of investors in case of Broker/Dealer failure (not, account volatility). The FDIC limit is $250,000 per person; whereas, the SIPC limit is $500,000 per person. The key to the concept of insuring deposits regarding both entities is not in the amount, but the "per person" clause. "Per person" is distinguished from "per account" in that a single person could have multiple accounts under their social security number. However, under that one social security number, the protection is maxed-out at the $250,000 (under FDIC) and $500,000 (under SIPC), respectively. When your client is effectively a different person, in that they have an account under their business Employer Identification Number, their Social Security number, their child's Social Security number (e.g. custodial account), and jointly with their spouse, they are insured up to the entity limits in each case.

EXAMPLE: John has 4 accounts listed under his social security number

- Savings: $68,500
- Checking: $16,200
- CD #1: $127,800
- CD #2: $144,375

The combined total value of his accounts is $356,875; however, he will only be insured under FDIC for $250,000. If he had restructured the accounts differently, each account would be covered up to $250,000.

EXAMPLE (Solution): John has 4 accounts listed in the following manner:

- Savings: $68,500 (under his social security number)
- Checking: $16,200 (under his business tax identification number)
- CD #1: $127,800 (held jointly with his wife)
- CD #2 $144,375 (held as a custodial account for his child)

The combined total value of his accounts is still $356,875; however, because John is effectively a different "person" in each account, each account would be covered up to $250,000.

This concept is important for your clients as their investment assets grow. A properly classified (i.e. brokerage, IRA, 529 Plan, UGMA, etc.) portfolio could open the door to your clients having millions of dollars invested with you under the protection of SIPC because the $500,000 limit would not be a roadblock.

<u>INTEREST</u>

Simple interest is defined as:

a) Interest on the original principal
b) Interest on the original principal in a specific period of time

$$\textbf{Simple Interest} = P \times I \times N$$

where:
P = principle
I= daily interest rate
N= number of days between payments

Compound interest is defined as:

a) Interest on both the original principal and the interest that has been earned
b) Interest on the original principal and earned interest in a specific period of time
c) Interest on the interest that has been earned

$$\textbf{Compound Interest} = [P\,(1+i)^n]\ -1$$
$$\textbf{Compound Interest} = P\,[(1+i)^n\ -1]$$

where:
P = principle
I= interest rate
N= number of compounding periods

Simple interest is interest on the original principal in a specific period of time. A simple return is where income accrues only on the principal and not on prior income. Simple returns are also referred to as non-compounded returns. When returns are non-compounded, the ending value of an investment can be computed as:

EndingValue = Beginning value × [1 + (rate of return × t)] (Equation A)

where t = the number of time periods

Compound interest is interest on both the original principal and the interest that has been credited throughout the period. In *compounding* returns, the income for each period is
added to the principal so that subsequent income is paid on both principal and accumulated income. When an investment is made for multiple periods and returns are compounded, then the ending value of the investment is computed as:

Ending Value = Beginning value × (1 + rate of return)t (Equation B)

EXAMPLE: A bank promises to pay 6 percent on a 5-year certificate of deposit. However, the interest rate will apply only to the principal, not to the accrued interest. If your client deposits
$10,000 in the account, the ending value is determined by using equation A, computed as:

Ending value = $10,000 x [1 + (.06 x 5)] = $13,000

EXAMPLE: Suppose in the previous example the bank changes its mind and agrees to let the interest be compounded. In this case, ending value is determined by using equation B:

Ending value = $10,000 x 1.065= $13,382.26

Thus, the compounding process has increased the ending value by $382.26.

Your worth as an advisor is predicated on the "value" that you present to your client. Your understanding of products and their growth nature are important to your client's financial well-being. As an example, an index annuity may offer options for the application of interest. In most cases, the option that allows for more frequent compounding results in a larger portfolio value.

INCOME versus NET WORTH

Income is a matter of earning capacity. Net Worth is the measure of a person's financial wealth. The net worth on a personal balance sheet is the difference between the total value of assets owned and the total amount of liabilities owed (e.g. Total Assets – Total Liabilities).

EXAMPLE: Ron and Pat Meller own a home they believe to be worth $200,000. The current balance on their mortgage is $150,000. There is $2,000 in their checking account. They own 100 shares of Eastman Kodak stock worth $50 per share. They both have IRAs. Ron's IRA is worth $28,000 and Pat's IRA is worth $12,000. They have $20,000 invested in a bond mutual fund. They own two automobiles, worth a combined value of $25,000. They have one car loan outstanding on which the current principal owed is $8,000. Ron has a pension at work that is currently worth $62,000. What is the Mellers net worth?

Don't confuse high-income with high-net worth. As you can guess, it is very possible that a person with a high-income can have a low net worth. This usually results from assets acquired through financing (i.e. cars, homes, boats, clothes, furniture, etc.) which increases their liabilities. Your guidance as an advisor is critical to the client's understanding of this concept, and more importantly… how to build their net worth and protect their earnings.

BUDGETING

A budget is an estimate of expected income and expenses for a defined period of time.

EXAMPLE OF A BUDGET

As you can tell from the spelling, BUDGET is not a "four-letter-word", so don't treat it as such. A budget is one of the most powerful tools at your client's disposal because it can help guide them in their decision-making. The budget helps them know how viable they are financially. If they like the results that they are seeing, they can continue spending money as status quo; however, if they don't like the results that they are seeing, they can use the budget to see where changes are necessary. A budget should have a "zero" balance. Why would that be preferable to showing a surplus? Ideally, you want to see a surplus in the budget, but when you shift that surplus to planned savings opportunities, the balance becomes "zero".

What you may find in your practice, as you conduct a financial needs analysis, is that clients will not include all of their expenses. While it is probably not intentional, often time irregular or small expenses are overlooked and/or underestimate. For example: you may forget to include drycleaning or you may underestimate what you spend on dining out. The bottom line is that the budget can be used effectively to see if the client is working with a surplus and is even a viable client for you.

The Impact of Behavioral Finance Biases on Your Practice

Behavioral Finance is a growing field of study that focuses on how human-nature plays into the financial decision-making process. In subsequent chapters we will see specific examples of how these biases play out, but for the time being, understand that your biases and those of your client can have a huge impact on their financial future.

Chapter 2

Financial Planning

Financial Planning and the Financial Planning Process

Personal financial planning is the process of managing your money to achieve short-term, intermediate-term and long-term financial goals. There are six steps in personal financial planning process.

Step 1. Determine Your Current Financial Situation.

Personal Financial statements are an integral part of the financial planning process because they allow you to have the ability to perform a ratio analysis. A ratio analysis allows you to determine your level of debt your savings amount, and your ability to fund short-term and long-term goals. There are two main personal financial statements to include; 1) the statement of financial position and 2) the statement of income and expenses.

Statement of Financial Position (Balance Sheet)

Statement of Financial Position Jim and Joan Martin Projected Balance Sheet as of 12/31/2020			
ASSETS		**LIABILITIES AND NET WORTH**	
Current Assets		**Current Liabilities**	
Checking Accounts	$17,250	Credit Card Balances	$25,470
Money Market Account	$13,569	**Total Current Liabilities**	**$25,470**
Total Current Assets	**$30,819**		
Investment Assets		**Long-Term Liabilities**	
401(k) Plan	$90,152	Mortgage Balance	$165,890
IRA	$18,423	Auto Loans	$15,623
CDs	$16,524	**Total Long Term Liabilities**	$181,513
Growth Mutual Fund	$19,654		
Stock Portfolio	$41,360		
Total Invested Assets	**$186,113**	**Total Liabilities**	**$206,983**
Personal Use Assets		**Total Net Worth**	**$300,588**
Personal Residence	$182,350		
Personal Property	$65,000		
Automobiles	$43,289		
Total Personal Use Assets	$290,639		
Total Assets	**$507,571**	**Total Liabilities and Net Worth**	**$507,571**

The statement of financial position is also known as a personal balance sheet of net worth statement. Cash and cash equivalents represent assets that are highly liquid, which means they are either cash or can be converted to cash (within the next 12 months) with little to no price concession from their current value. Cash and cash equivalents also represent very safe investments that are unlikely to lose value.

Typical assets included in the category of cash and cash equivalents are:

- Cash
- Checking Accounts
- Money Market Accounts
- Savings Accounts
- Certificates of deposit (maturity is less than 12 months).

Since cash and cash equivalents represents highly liquid safe investments, it is important to the client's financial position and financial performance to maintain sufficient levels of cash and cash equivalents tc meet liabilities that are due within the next 12 months.

Investment Assets include appreciating assets or those being held to accomplish one or more financial goals. Investment assets are listed on the balance sheet at the current fair market values. Typical assets included in this category are:

- Retirement accounts
- Brokerage accounts
- Education savings accounts
- Cash value is life insurance
- Business ownership interest and
- The vested portion of any pension plan
- Annuities

Personal use assets are those assets that maintain the clients' lifestyle. Example of assets included in personal use assets are:

- Personal residences
- Automobiles
- Furniture
- Clothing
- Boats
- Jet ski
- Vacation homes
- Electronics (television, stereo, iPod, etc.)
- Collectibles (art, antiques)

Liabilities represent financial obligations that you owe to creditors. To satisfy a liability, either a client-owned asset or some other economic benefit must be transferred to the creditor. A liability may be either a legal obligation or moral obligation that resulted from a past transaction A legal obligation may be a mortgage or a car payment.

Short-term liabilities represent those obligations that are "current" in nature that are due or expected to be paid within the next 12 months (o less than 12 months). Example of liabilities that are included in short-term or current liabilities are:

- Electric, gas, water, garbage, and sewage bills incurred, but not yet paid.
- Principal portion of any debt obligations due within the next 12 months
- Unpaid credit card bills
- Outstanding medical expenses
- Insurance premiums due
- Unpaid taxes

Long-term liabilities are financial obligation owed that are due and expected to be paid beyond the next 12 months. Long-term liabilities are usually that result of major financial purchases and resulting obligations that are amortized over multiple years.

- Primary residence loans
- Vacation home loans
- Automobile loans
- Student loans, any other of loan or promissory note
- Business loans

When reporting the outstanding balance of a loan, the current portion of the liability should be reported separately from the long-term portion of the liability. This allows you to make a comparison between current assets and current liabilities and to evaluate your liquidity status and ability to meet short-term financial obligations.

Your net worth as reflected on the balance sheet represents the amount of total equity (assets-liabilities = net worth) you have accumulated as of the date of the balance sheet. When evaluating your financial position, net worth is an important consideration because it represents an absolute dollar amount reflective of a client's financial position. A positive net worth may imply that you have done a good job of saving, investing, and managing debt. A negative net worth implies that you are insolvent and potentially facing bankruptcy.

Statement of Income and Expenses

Statement of Income and Expenses James and Christina Williams Statement of Income and Expenses for 2020	
CASH INFLOWS	
Salaries	
John's Salary	$85,000
Barbara's Salary	$52,000
Total Cash Inflows	$137,000
CASH RESERVES	
Savings	
Employee-Elective deferral	$15,963
Total Savings	
Ordinary Living expenses	
Debt Payment	
Credit Card Payments	$5,230
Mortgage Loan	$15,666
Auto Loans	$3,200
Total Debt Payments	$19,389
Insurance Premiums	
Life Insurance	$1,235
Health Insurance	$400
Auto Insurance	$600
Homeowners Insurance	$1,250
Total Insurance Premiums	$3,485
Charitable Contributions	$520
Tuition & Education Expenses	$12,000
Entertainment & Vacations	$1,500
Taxes	
Federal Income Taxes	$1,320
State Income Taxes	$2,100
social security Taxes	$6,085
Property Tax (Residence)	$2,500
Total Taxes	$12,005

Total Cash Outflows	$64,862
NET CASH FLOW	$72,138

A statement of income and expenses (income statement) is a representation of income (inflows)
earned, and expenses incurred for a client during a specified period of time. Typically **income** includes the following items:

- Salary
- Interest
- Dividend
- Business Income
- Money received from retirement account
- Pension payments
- Alimony received

Expenses (outflows) include

- Utilities (electricity or gas)
- Taxes
- Insurance
- Telephone bills
- Cell phone bill
- Cable bill
- Water bill

In addition to expenses clients also contribute some of their income to savings (outflows).

A **budget** is an estimation of the revenue and expenses over a specified future period of time. A budget can be made for a person, family, group of people, business, government, country, multinational organization or just about anything else that makes and spends money. A budget is a microeconomic concept that shows the tradeoff made when one good i exchanged for another. Budgets allows a client and advisor to evaluate the clients spending and savings habits. The **emergency fund** helps you withstand a sudden negative financial disruption of income or extraordinary expense. The emergency fund is comprised of cash and cash equivalents. Emergency funds should generally be three to six months' worth of non-discretional cash flows to accommodate unemployment, Loss of significant assets, or other unexpected major expenditures. Non-discretionary cash flows are those expenses that exist even if a job or income source is lost. Non-discretionary cash flows are typically fixed expenses. Examples of non-discretionary expenses includes, all debt payments (mortgage, car loan, student loan, credit cards) utilities, insurance premiums, property taxes and food.

- **3 months** is generally used when there are two working spouses or a second source of income.
- **6 months** is generally used when the client is single or married and only one of the spouses works.

The **debt management** section of ratio analysis provides insight into how well the client is managing debt and the quality of that debt.

- Consumer debt payments should not exceed **36%** of take home pay.

The banking industry has established certain criteria when deciding to extend credit for a mortgage. The front-end housing to debt ratio is the amount of income and housing debt that a client is carrying to decide whether a mortgage is appropriate and affordable. If a borrower meets criteria 1, he/she likely will qualify for a traditional mortgage loan at a favorable rate.

- The monthly front-end housing costs should not exceed **28%** of gross income or one week's take home pay and it is computed as housing cost divided by gross income.

Hosing cost equals **PITI** which is principal, interest, taxes, and insurance. Gross income is gross pay before taxes and other income sources with a history of at least two prior years.

The back-end housing ratio is also referred the back-end **debt to income ratio**. This ratio was established by the banking industry to determine if the total amount of debt that a client is carrying is appropriate for a given level of income. If the back- end housing ratio i met, the borrower will likely qualify for a conventional loan at a favorable rate. The formula for the back-end ratio is housing cost plus other debt payments divided by gross income.

Debt to income ratio = $\frac{housing\ costs + other\ debt}{gross\ income}$

All other debts include car loan payment, boat loan payments, student loan payments, credit card payments, principle and interest on vacation or second home and any other monthly recurring debt.

- Monthly payments on all debt should not exceed **36%** of monthly gross income.

Saving is a very important part of financial planning. You should consciously plan to save a certain portion of their monthly income. Thi concept has been described for many years as "paying yourself first". The common savings percentage cited is 10%. Financial planners can use a client's goals to determine an appropriate level of savings.

Step 2. Develop Financial Goals: Once you have evaluated you current financial situation, you are ready to move forward in th financial planning process. The second step is developing your financi goals. Setting goals will give you a direction for your plan and destination toward which you want to head.

Setting goals are important and often used to measure success. However, simply setting goals does not ensure you will someday accomplish them. Achieving goals requires establishing a plan. Planning is important to ensure a direction for your day-to-day actions. Being deliberate about establishing a plan can help guide the decisions you make to aid you in reaching your goals. The further your goals are from today, the more important it is to have a plan to ensure your success in reaching those goals. **The personal financial planning life cycle** reflects the changes that occur over a person's lifetime. Throughout thi lifecycle, individuals have to continually refine their personal financial plan to meet these ever-changing financial goals. In childhood and adolescence, individuals are dependent on their parents or guardians for support. They typically have little or no income, and their expenses are subsumed within the overall household expenses. Planning becomes more complicated in the early twenties. Some individuals move directly from high school into careers and begin to accumulate savings and debt. In their late twenties they may marry and enjoy life with two incomes and no children. As they being to have children their financial goals shift to protection and increasing their standard of living. In their forties and fifties, they focus on putting their children through college and planning for retirement.

Types of Financial Goals

- *Short-term goals* are those to be achieved within the next year or so, such as saving for an annual vacation or paying off small debts.
- *Intermediate goals* have a time frame of two to five years.
- *Long-term goals* involve financial plans that may be more than five years off, such as retirement and college savings.
- *Consumable-product goals* usually occur on a periodic basis involving items used up relatively quickly, such as food, clothing, or entertainment spending.
- *Durable-product goals* usually involve infrequent, expensive items, such as appliances, motor vehicles, and sporting equipment. Most durable goals consist of tangible items. In contrast, however, many people overlook *intangible goals*. These goals may relate to personal relationships, health, education, and leisure. Goal setting for these life circumstances is also necessary for a person's overall well-being Factors.

Step 3. Identify Alternative Courses of Action: Generally, your alternative courses of actions will fall into one of two categories: reallocating existing resources, or generating new ones. Existing resources can be utilized by earmarking current savings or shifting current allocations as in the example above. Generating new resources may require changing jobs to improve your wage outlook, taking on additional hours or investing your savings more aggressively to generate higher rates of return.

Step 4. Evaluate Your Alternatives: Once you have given serious thought to the options available that could lead you to your goals, you may begin to realize just how many options there are. When evaluating your alternatives, also be sure to consider the opportunity costs of what you will forego to pursue your goal through each course of action. Adequately evaluating each of your options can help to ensure you select the best course of action to accomplish your financial goals.

Step 5. Create and Implement Your Financial Action Plan: As you put together your financial plan, it's important to look at the entire picture. Having identified options for reaching your goals and having weighed each strategy, it's now easier to look at the cost of your goals in terms of your current situation. This can help you to prioritize your goals as you consider how much it will cost you to implement each one. Finalizing your plan will require you to make decisions as to which goals to pursue and the best courses of action to take. All of this will have to be weighed in terms of your current situation and practical predictions for your future to maintain realistic and obtainable goals.

Once you've gone through the effort of creating your plan, discipline is paramount. After mapping your path to your goals, it important that you follow that path. Be conscious about establishing actionable steps you can take to lead you to success when creating your plan. Having concrete steps to take will help you ensure you are doing what you need to do to stay on track to accomplish your goals.

Step 6. Review and Revise Your Plan: The final step in developing a personal financial plan is perhaps the most important. You may have done your due diligence at each step along the way and created a solid financial plan. However, one fact remains: life happens. For this reason, it is important to review your plan often and revise it as needed. Reviewing your financial plan can help you to gauge your progress toward meeting your goals. Original strategies may not be having the expected results and may require adjustment to help you meet your goals.

Factors Influencing Personal Financial Planning

Personal Factors Influencing Personal Financial Planning

The financial planning environment is affected by life situation, personal values (behavioral finance), and economic factors. The personal factors include your age, income, size of household, and your attitudes and beliefs. Your life situation is affected by various personal events. Values are personal beliefs and ideas that a person considers correct, desirable, and important. An individual's values and beliefs have evolved into the study of behavioral finance. **Behavioral finance** is a relatively new field that seeks to combine behavioral and cognitive psychological theory with conventional economics and finance to provide explanations for why people make irrational financial decisions. **Attitudes** are byproducts of our **values**. Attitudes are expressed through physical actions or verbal communication. Values guide our belief system and our attitudes are an expression of those value. Investors come from different cultural and family backgrounds which shape their belief system and help guide their attitudes toward investing and saving. Investors' perceptions about the value of financial planning can be manifested in their risk capacity, lifecycle and age, and their knowledge or experience.

- **Risk capacity/tolerance:** Younger clients possess a longer time horizon and have a great ability to recover from an investment mistake and are usually more risk seeking. Older clients tend to be more conservative and are more risk adverse due to their inability to recover from poor investment performance because of a shorter time horizon before retirement; but that should be considered a generalization and not "gospel".
- **Life cycle and age**: Younger clients tend to have shorter attention spans, while older clients tend to be more attentive and take planning for the future more serious. Once more, these should be taken as generalizations.
- **Knowledge or experience:** experience investors are sometimes more resistant to financial advice because of the development of preconceived benefits or shortcomings.

Financial planners must be aware of the fact that they may inject their own belief system into the plan which may not always be in the best interest of the client. Financial planners need to possess empathy and self-awareness.

Biases predispose individuals to commit certain errors.

- **Confirmation bias**: occur when people attach too much importance to information that supports their views
- **Survivor bias:** investors believe that they survived a downturn in the market because of their superior skills in choosing the right securities.
- **Hindsight bias:** a belief after-the-fact that past events were or should have been predicted.
- **Overreaction bias:** investors sometimes overreact to new information.
- **Availability bias:** Causes individuals to overestimate risks when events are easy to imagine or recall.
- **Familiarity bias**: individuals tend to fear unfamiliar risk more than familiar risk
- **Overconfidence bias**: occurs when investors make many mistakes but still believe they are above average investors.

Investors in financial markets also tend to think as a group and make irrational decisions. It is almost uncanny how an event can trigger so many market participants to unconsciously react in the same ways. **Behavioral finance** is the theory that attempts to explain a response to this strange behavior. The theory attempts to explain how investors process events and formulate decisions. Theoretically, understanding behavioral finance allows other investors to predict market movements and profit from them. Below are a few of the theories related to behavioral finance:

- **Anchoring:** describes and individual's tendency to rely on the first piece of information they receive.
- **Recency:** a behavioral finance term that the most recent return leaves a larger psychological impact than earlier returns.

- **Mental Accounting:** system of different values and preferences that a person places on a given dollar amount in different situations.
- **Planning fallacy:** is a condition when individuals underestimate the length of time it will take to complete a task or plan.
- **Herd mentality**: Investors are sometimes influenced by peers and may follow others with regards to investment choices
- **Engels's law**: states that the percentage of income allocated for food purchases decreases as income rises.

Economic Factors Influencing Personal Financial Planning

Supply represents the quantity of a good offered to the market. The law of supply demonstrates the quantity supplied or sold at a given price. As the price increases the quantity supplied increases which accounts for the upward sloping curve (Supply curve). The upward sloping curve depicts a direct relationship. **Demand** refers to the quantity or a product or service desired by willing buyers. The law of demand states that if all other

things are held constant, less will be demanded as the price increases (demand curve). The downward sloping curve depicts an inverse relationship. The equilibrium point is the point where supply equals demand.

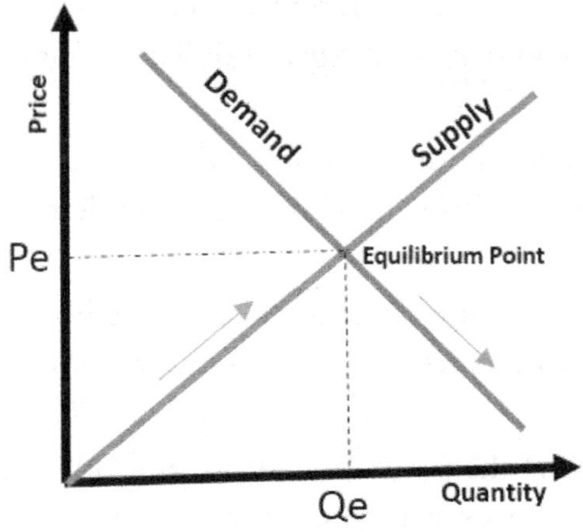

Elasticity is an economic concept that describes the change in demand as a result in a change in price. Elasticities greater than one are called "elastic," elasticities less than one are "inelastic," and elasticities equal to one are "unit elastic."

$$Elasticity = \frac{\%change\ in\ quantity}{\%\ change\ in\ price}$$

Example: Consumer demand for beans at $5 per pound results in 30 bags being sold, and a drop in price to $4 per pound results in 32 bags being sold. Based on this result, one could conclude that the demand is **inelastic.**

Rationale: $\frac{2/62}{-\frac{1}{9}} = -.2907$

Fiscal policy is the use of government spending and taxation to influence the economy. When the government decides on the goods and services it purchases, the transfer payments it distributes, or the taxes it collects, it is engaging in fiscal policy. The primary economic impact of any change in the government budget is felt by particular groups—a tax cut for families with children, for example, raises their disposable income. Discussions of fiscal policy, however, generally focus on the effect of changes in the government budget on the overall economy. Using fiscal policy congress seeks to support economic growth and full employment. The three tools of fiscal policy are taxation, spending, and debt management. Fiscal policy is said to be tight or contractionary when revenue is higher than spending (i.e., the government budget is in surplus) and loose or expansionary when spending is higher than revenue (i.e., the budget is in deficit). Often, the focus is not on the level of the deficit, but on the *change* in the deficit. Thus, a reduction of the deficit from $200 billion to $100 billion is said to be contractionary fiscal policy, even though the budget is still in deficit. **Monetary policy,** measures efforts employed by governments to influence economic activity, specifically by manipulating the supply of money and credit and by altering rates of interest. The usual goals of monetary policy are to achieve or maintain full employment, to achieve or maintain a high rate of economic growth, and to stabilize prices and wages. Until the early 20th century, monetary policy was thought by most experts to be of little use in influencing the economy. Inflationary trends after World War II, however, caused governments to adopt measures that reduced inflation by restricting growth in the money supply. Using monetary policy, the Federal Reserve (FED) seeks to support economic growth, full employment and price stability. The Fed controls money supply with four tools: reserve requirements; discount rate; open market operations; and interest rates on required balances and excess reserves. Increases in the money supply decreases interest rates; and decreases in the money supply increases interest rates. The **first** is by far the most important. By buying or selling government securities (usually bonds), the Fed—or a central bank—affects the money supply and interest rates. If, for example, the Fed buys government securities, it pays with a check drawn on itself. This action creates money in the form of additional deposits from the sale of the securities by commercial banks. By adding to the cash reserves of the commercial banks, then, the

Fed enables those banks to increase their lending capacity. Consequently, the additional demand for government bonds bids up their price and thus reduces their yield (i.e., interest rates). The purpose of this operation is to ease the availability of credit and to reduce interest rates, which thereby encourages businesses to invest more and consumers to spend more. The selling of government securities by the Fed achieves the opposite effect of contracting the money supply and increasing interest rates.

The **second** tool is the discount rate, which is the interest rate at which the Fed (or a central bank) lends to commercial banks. An increase in the discount rate reduces the amount of lending made by banks. In most countries the discount rate is used as a signal, in that a change in the discount rate will typically be followed by a similar change in the interest rates charged by commercial banks. The **third** tool deals with changes in the reserve requirements. Commercial banks by law hold a specific percentage of their deposits and required reserves with the Fed (or a central bank). These are held either in the form of non-interest-bearing reserves or as cash. This reserve requirement acts as a brake on the lending operations of the commercial banks: by increasing or decreasing this reserve-ratio requirement, the Fed can influence the amount of money available for lending and hence the money supply. This tool is rarely used, however, because it is so blunt. The Bank of England and most other central banks also employ a number of other tools, such as "treasury directive" regulation of installment purchasing and "special deposits."

Economic indicators provide insight about the direction of the economy. There are three types of economic indicators; leading, lagging and coincident.

Leading indicators A measurable economic factor that changes before the economy starts to follow a particular pattern or trend. Leading indicators are used to predict changes in the economy, but are not always accurate. Bond yields are typically a good leading indicator of the market because traders anticipate and speculate trends in the economy. Common leading economic indicators include:

- Average weekly work hours in manufacturing

- Housing permits
- Stock prices
- building permits (new private housing)
- industrial production rates
- money supply
- S&P 500
- average of weekly unemployment insurance claims

Lagging indicators: A measurable economic factor that changes after the economy has already begun to follow a particular pattern or trend. Lagging indicators confirm long-term trends, but do not predict them. Interest rates (especially the prime interest rate) are a good lagging indicator; rates change after severe market changes. Common lagging indicators include:

- Average length unemployment
- Labor cost per unit of manufacturing output
- Average prime rate
- Consumer price index
- Corporate profit

Coincident indicators: An economic factor that varies directly and simultaneously with the business cycle, thus indicating the current state of the economy. Common coincident indicators include:

- Unemployment rate
- Personal income levels
- Industrial production
- Inventory/sales ratio

Gross Domestic Product (GDP). This economic indicator measures the country's total output. This includes everything produced by all the people and all the companies in the country.

The components of GDP are:

- Personal Consumption Expenditures
- Business Investment
- Government Spending
- Net exports = (Exports minus Imports).

GDP standard formula is C + I + G + (X-M).

Nominal GDP is GDP evaluated at current market prices. Therefore, nominal GDP will include all of the changes in market prices that have occurred during the current year due to **inflation** or **deflation**. Inflation is defined as a rise in the overall price level, and deflation is defined as a fall in the overall price level. In order to deviate from changes in the overall price level, another measure of GDP called **real GDP** is often used.

Real GDP: To compare Gross Domestic Product from one year to another, it's important to take out the effects of inflation. To do this, the Bureau of Economic Analysis (BEA) calculates real GDP. It does this b using a price deflator, which tells you how much prices have changed since a **base year**. The BEA multiplies the deflator by the nominal GDP.

Chapter 3

Education Funding

Education Needs Analysis

It is best to save for education costs prior to the need: education expenses include tuition, books, lodging, transportation, insurance, meals, entertainment, fraternity/sorority, computer, Internet access and other miscellaneous items. Calculating the amount of money that needs to be saved on a regular basis to help cover the cost of sending a student to college is a four-step process:

- **Estimate education costs in current dollars**
  The starting point for estimating future education costs is finding an appropriate figure to represent current costs. The appropriate figure will depend on whether the student in question is likely to attend a public or private institution, a particular school and what, if any, the student will be expected to contribute.
- **Project future education costs in inflated dollars**
  Use time value of money calculations to project what college costs are likely to be when a child of a particular age will be ready to enroll. A component of this calculation will be an inflation rate at which college costs are expected to increase. Historically, the tuition inflation rate has exceeded the overall inflation rate.
- **Determine the required lump-sum investment**
  This calculation solving for present value determines how much would need to be set aside now to ensure sufficient funds are available when a student enrolls.
- **Calculate the required periodic investment**
  Most parents will not have sufficient funds set aside now to finance a child's education without further investing.

Education Savings Vehicles

529 Plan

Qualified Tuition Program (also known as Section 529 plans) - Program run by a state, state agency or educational institution that allows for prepayment of qualified education expenses or contributions to a tax-free account for education savings. Earnings are tax free. Comes in two varieties: the college savings plan and the prepaid tuition program.

Prepaid tuition plan - parent or other account owner contributes cash for beneficiary and the contribution purchases tuition credits at current tuition rates. Prepaid tuition plans allow contributors to prepay tuition today at a particular school for an individual in the future. The plan will lock in today's prices but subjects the particular plan beneficiary to man risks. The main risks are that the beneficiary may choose a school different from the one named in the plan or may not be accepted into the school named in the plan.

College savings plan - parent or other account owner contributes on behalf of beneficiary with contributions invested according to the term's investment options.

Contributions are not deductible.

- Tax-free distributions for qualified expenses.
- Applies to tuition, fees, books, supplies, equipment, room and board if at least a half-time student and expenses for special needs services.
- Covers undergraduate and graduate education.
- Qualifies for $15,000 annual gift tax exclusion for 2020.
- Contributor may prorate contribution over five years for purposes of claiming gift tax exclusion. Allows for one-time contribution of $75,000 ($15,000 per year times five years) for a single beneficiary (IRS, 2020).
- No income phaseout.
- May be eligible for state tax deduction.
- Nonqualified distributions subject to regular income tax plus additional 10% tax.
- Transfers between beneficiaries belonging to the same family allowed.

Custodial Accounts (UGMA and UTMA)
An account created at a bank, brokerage firm or mutual fund company that is managed by an adult for a minor that is under the age of 18 to 21 (depending on state legislation).

Uniform Gifts to Minors Act (UGMA) and Uniform Transfers to Minor Act (UTMA) are custodial assets. They allow parents the option to put assets in a custodial account for a child. If the child is younger than age 19 (or 24 if full-time student), a portion of the child's unearned income (i.e., interest and dividends) may be taxed at the income tax rate of the parents (also known as the Kiddie Tax). Custodial account assets are considered an asset of the child and are considered in the determination of financial aid.

The Uniform Gift to Minors Act (UGMA) established a simple way for a minor to own securities without requiring the services of an attorney to prepare trust documents or the court appointment of a trustee. The terms of this trust are established by a state statute instead of a trust document. The Uniform Transfer to Minors Act (UTMA) is similar, but also allows minors to own other types of property, such as real estate, fine art, patents and royalties, and for the transfers to occur through inheritance.

To establish a custodial account, the donor must appoint a custodian (trustee) and provide the name and social security number of the minor. The donor irrevocably gifts the money to the trust. The money then belongs to the minor but is controlled by the custodian until the minor reaches the age of trust termination. The custodian has the fiduciary responsibility to manage the money in a prudent fashion for the benefit of the minor. Custodial accounts are most often established at banks and brokerages.

Any money in custodial accounts for which you are the custodian will be counted as part of your taxable estate if you are the legal guardian of the child and the child has not yet reached the age of trust termination.

The income from a custodial account must be reported on the child's tax return and is taxed at the child's rate, subject to the Kiddie Tax rules.

The parent is responsible for filing an income tax return on behalf of the child. There is no special tax treatment for UGMA accounts. Children aged 14 and older must sign their own tax returns. .

Neither the donor nor the custodian can place any restrictions on the use of the money when the minor becomes an adult. At that time the child can use the money for any purpose whatsoever without requiring permission of the custodian, so there's no guarantee that the child will use the money for his or her education. Also, since UGMA and UTMA accounts are in the name of a single child, the funds are not transferrable to another beneficiary.

Impact on Student Aid Eligibility

For financial aid purposes, custodial accounts are considered assets of the student. This means that custodial bank and brokerage accounts have a high impact on financial aid eligibility.

Coverdell Education Savings Account

Coverdell contribution limit $2,000 per year per beneficiary. Funds must be used by age 30. No contribution past the 18th birthday. Owner may change beneficiary. It can be used for college, secondary, or primary education. Generally considered to be a parent asset for financial aid purposes. There is a high phase-out contribution eligibility.

- Contributions not allowed once beneficiary reaches age 18 (unless a special needs beneficiary).
- Tax-free distributions for qualified expenses.
- Covers undergraduate, graduate and K-12 education.
- Applies to tuition, fees, books, supplies, equipment, payments to qualified tuition programs and special needs services.
- Assets must be distributed by age 30 unless beneficiary has special needs.
- Nonqualified distributions subject to regular income tax plus additional 10% tax.
- Income phaseouts for contributions: $95,000 to $110,000 (single); $190,000 to $220,000 (joint returns) for 2020.

Savings Bonds

U.S. Savings Bonds
The main types of non-marketable government bonds are Series EE, HH, and I savings bonds.

Series EE Bonds: Series EE Bonds are 30-year investments issued in denominations ranging from $50 to $10,000. They are purchased for half (50%) of their face value at financial institutions that are qualified as savings bond agents. (For investors who have purchased Series EE bonds since May 1, 1997, and have held the bonds for at least five years, the interest rate is equivalent to 90% of the average yield on five-year Treasury bonds based on the previous six months.) The rate is reset twice a year - on May 1 and November 1 - and is therefore variable.

Series HH Bonds: Series HH Bonds are 20-year investments that pay semiannual interest and have face values ranging from $500 to $10,000. The only way to acquire HH bonds is to exchange at least $500 in EE bonds. The interest on both Series EE and HH bonds is federally taxable but free of state and local taxes. Taxes on the interest of Series EE bonds can be deferred until the bond matures or is cashed in.

Series I Bonds: The U.S. government began issuing Series I bonds in September 1998. These bonds are indexed for inflation and are available in the same denominations as EE bonds. Unlike EE bonds, they are sold at face value, and their interest rate is reset semiannually based on the rate of inflation. Interest on I-bonds is paid over 30 years and is reinvested back into the principal of the bond as long as the bond is held. Series I-bonds are free from state and local taxation. Moreover, federal taxes are deferred until the bonds are redeemed or mature. I-bonds are partially or wholly tax-exempt if used for higher education, making them good candidates for college savings.

Interest earned on savings bonds used to cover qualified education expenses is not subject to tax.

- Limit is equal to amount of qualified education expenses.
- Covers only tuition and required enrollment fees.
- Tax-free transfers to Coverdell Education Savings Accounts and 529 plans also allowed.

- Applies to undergraduate and graduate education.
- Only series EE bonds issued after 1989 or all series I-bonds qualify.
- The bond owner must be an adult at least 24 years old before the bond's issue date.
- Income phaseouts: $97,350 (single); $153,550 (joint returns) in 2019.

Financial Aid

Free Application for Federal Student Aid (FAFSA)

FAFSA is the application used by nearly all colleges and universities to determine eligibility for federal, state, and college-sponsored financial aid, including grants, educational loans, and work-study programs. Known commonly as the FAFSA, the Free Application for Federal Student Aid is the starting point for college financial aid. The form is produced and processed by the U.S. Department of Education. Information disclosed on the form is used by colleges and state agencies to help determine the size of financial aid awards.

Grants

Grants and Scholarships - Grants do not have to be paid back and are awarded by federal and state governments and individual institutions. Scholarships are usually based on merit.

- **Federal Pell Grants** are outright gifts from the government based on the students' need and the cost of attending the chosen school. Only undergraduate students who have not previously received a bachelors' degree eligible for the grants. The maximum amount of award changes each year depending on program funding. The Federal Pell Grant program is the largest need-based student aid program.
- **Supplemental Educational Opportunity Grant** - A federal grant program for low-income students. The government distributes funds to individual schools, which are responsible for awarding grants of up to $4,000 per year. The Federal Supplements Education Opportunity Grant (SEOG) Program is

another grant program for undergraduates with exceptional financial need. This program is managed by colleges instead of the federal government. Students are automatically considered when they submit a FAFSA form.

Scholarships

- **Merit Based Scholarships -** Exceptional high school students are often awarded merit based educational financial aid in the form of scholarships that do not have to be repaid. Qualifying for such scholarships can depend on a student's high school performance or on their scores on commonly accepted scholastic aptitude tests, such as the SAT Reasoning Test or the ACT.

Work Study

- **Work Study Plans -** Some students may wish to apply to their educational establishment to see if employment opportunities are available for them to earn money to put toward educational expenses while they study. The U.S. Federal Government currently offers a 60 percent wage subsidy to employers of students engaged in work-study programs.

Internships

- **Internships and Apprenticeships** On the job training opportunities are often available in the form of internship for white collar jobs and apprenticeships for blue collar jobs. These educational programs are typically run half time during the school year to accommodate the need to attend classes, and full time during the summer. Although usually low paying, they allow students to obtain valuable hands-on experience in their chosen field and may even result in a job offer from the company they participated in the program with.
-

Tax Credits/income Tax Strategies

Federal law grants a number of tax benefits to help ease the costs of higher education. Careful review is required to help determine which ones are best to claim by a particular individual or family. As a general rule, a taxpayer cannot claim more than one benefit for the same education expense. Benefits generally can be used in combination for separate expenses.

American Opportunity Credit

American Opportunity Tax Credit is a credit for qualified education expenses paid for an eligible student for the first four years of higher education. You can get a maximum annual credit of $2,500 per eligible student. If the credit brings the amount of tax you owe to zero, you can have 40 percent of any remaining amount of the credit (up to $1,000) refunded to you.

- Applies to tuition and required enrollment fees as well as books and supplies.
- Covers only first four years of undergraduate education.
- Student must be enrolled at half-time in degree program.
- No felony drug convictions of student.
- Income phaseouts: $80,000 to $90,000 (single); $160,000 to $180,000 (joint returns) for year 2020.

The following expenses do not qualify:

- Room and board
- Transportation
- Insurance
- Medical expenses
- Student fees unless required as a condition of enrollment or attendance
- Same expenses paid with tax-free educational assistance
- Same expenses used for any other tax deduction, credit or educational benefit

Lifetime Learning Credit

The Lifetime Learning Credit is for qualified tuition and related expense paid for eligible students enrolled in an eligible educational institution. This credit can help pay for undergraduate, graduate and professional degree courses--including courses to acquire or improve job skills. There is no limit on the number of years you can claim the credit. Tax credit equal to 20% of tuition and related expenses up to a maximum of $2,000 per year per family.

- Applies only to tuition and required enrollment fees (not books or supplies).

- Covers undergraduate and graduate education as well as higher education courses intended to acquire or improve job skills.
- Available for an unlimited number of years for one or more courses.
- Felony drug conviction rule does not apply.
- Income phaseouts: $59,000 to $68,000 (single); $118,00 to $136,000 (joint returns) in 2020.

Tuition and Fees Deduction

A deduction of up to $4,000 for qualified expenses that reduces income subject to income tax.

- Applies only to tuition and required enrollment fees.
- Covers both undergraduate and graduate education.
- Cannot claim both deduction and education credit for same student in same year.
- An adjustment to income that can be claimed even if taxpayer does not itemize deductions.
- Income phaseouts: $65,000 to $80,000 (single); $130,000 to $160,000 (joint returns) for 2020.

Student Loan Interest Deduction

A deduction of up to $2,500 on student loan interest paid in a tax year.

- Applies to tuition, fees, books, supplies, equipment, room and board, transportation and other necessary expenses.
- Covers undergraduate and graduate education.
- Student must have been enrolled at least half time in degree program.
- Covers lifetime of the loan.
- Income phaseouts: $70,000 to $50,000 (single); $140,000 to $170,000 (joint returns) for 2020.

Educational Exception To 10% Penalty on Early IRA Distributions

Allows IRA owners to withdraw funds before retirement to cover education expenses without being subject to the 10% early withdrawal penalty.

- Withdrawal may be subject to regular income tax.

- Limit is equal to amount of qualified education expenses.
- Covers books, supplies, equipment, room and board for at least half-time student and expenses for special needs services.
- Applies to undergraduate and graduate education.
- No income phaseouts.

Employer-Provided Educational Assistance

Tax-free educational assistance benefits include payments for tuition, fees and similar expenses, books, supplies, and equipment. Education generally includes any form of instruction or training that improves or develops your capabilities. The payments do not have to be for work-related courses or courses that are part of a degree program.

- Exclusion is limited to $5,250 per year (2020).
- Covers tuition, fees, books, supplies and equipment.
- Applies to undergraduate and graduate education.
- No income phaseouts.

Business Deduction for Worked-Related Education

Qualified expenses for work-related education may be deducted.

- Covers tuition, fees, transportation and other necessary expenses.
- Education required by employer or law or that maintains or improves job skills qualifies.
- Cannot be to meet minimum education requirements of present trade or business.
- Cannot qualify you for new trade or business.
- For employees, deduction is subject to 2% floor for miscellaneous expenses.
- For self-employed individuals, deduction is taken from self-employment income.

Scholarships, Fellowships, Grants and Tuition Reductions

These forms of educational assistance are tax free if they meet certain requirements.

- Assistance received for tuition, fees, books, supplies and equipment qualify for tax-free treatment.
- Payments for room, board and travel are taxable.

- Covers undergraduate, graduate and K-12 education.
- Student must be enrolled in a degree or vocational program.
- Students who qualify for tuition reduction or study tuition free receive these benefits tax free if they are received from an eligible educational institution and used at an eligible institution.

Education Financing

Loans

Federal Student Loans - There are three main types of federal student loans which are Perkins loans, subsidized Stafford Loans and unsubsidized Stafford Loans.

- **Perkins Loans** - Need-based loans awarded to students with the highest need. Features very low interest rate. Student not required to make any loan payments while in school. The federal Perkins Loan Program is a federally funded program administered by college. The program provides loans of up to $5,500 per year for undergraduate students and $8,000 per year for graduate students, with cumulative limits of $27,500 for undergraduate loans and $60,000 for undergraduate and graduate loans combined. Characteristics of a Perkins Loan include a 5% fixed interest rate, deferred repayment, a 9-month grace period, and a maximum of 10 years to repay the loan. Students are automatically considered if they complete a FASFA. The interest is subsidized by the federal government while the student is in school and during the 9-month deferral period.

Subsidized and unsubsidized loans are federal student loans for eligible students to help cover the cost of higher education at a four-year college or university, community college, or trade, career, or technical school. The U.S. Department of Education offers eligible students at participating schools Direct Subsidized Loans and Direct Unsubsidized Loans. (Some people refer to these loans as Stafford Loans or Direct Stafford Loans.)

- **Subsidized Stafford Loans** - Need-based loans, also with very low interest rates. The federal government pays the interest on the loan while child is in school and during six-month grace period following graduation.

- **Unsubsidized Stafford Loans** - Not based on financial need. Student is responsible for paying interest on the loan that accrues during in-school period. Student may pay interest while in school or have the interest added to the principal upon graduation.

Interest rates on Federal Stafford Loans are fixed. The 2020 fixed interest rates will be 2.75% on the Federal Stafford loan for undergraduate students, 4.3% for the Federal Stafford loan for graduate students and 5.3% for the Federal Grad PLUS and Federal Parent PLUS loans.

The loan fees are 1.062% for Federal Direct Stafford loans and 4.248% for Federal PLUS loans from October 1, 2018 through September 30, 2019. The fees will drop to 1.059% and 4.236% on October 1, 2019 through September 30, 2020.

Other Student Loan Options

- **Private student loans** - Many lenders offer private education loans to students. These loans are not subsidized and usually carry a higher interest rate than federal need-based loans.
- **College-sponsored loans** - Some colleges operate their own loan funds. Interest rates may be lower than federal student loans.

Loan Repayment Grace Period

The grace period is a set period of time after you graduate, leave school, or drop below half-time enrollment before you must begin repayment on your loan. The grace period gives you time to get financially settled and to select your repayment plan. Not all federal student loans have a grace period. Note that for most loans, interest will accrue during your grace period.

- Direct Subsidized Loans, Direct Unsubsidized Loans, Subsidized Federal Stafford Loans, and Unsubsidized Federal Stafford Loans have a 6-month grace period before payments are due.

- PLUS loans have no grace period. They enter repayment once they are fully disbursed but may be eligible for a *deferment.* Contact your loan servicer for more information.
- If you received a *Federal Perkins Loan*, check with the school where you received your loan.

Circumstances that may change your grace period include the following:

- Active duty military—If you are called to active military duty for more than 30 days before the end of your grace period, you will receive the full 6-month grace period when you return from active duty.
- Returning to school before the end of your loan's grace period—If you reenroll in school at least half-time before the end of your grace period, you will receive the full six-month grace period when you stop attending school or drop below half-time enrollment (other conditions apply).
- Loan consolidation—If you consolidate your loans during your grace period, you will give up the remainder of your grace period and begin repayment after your *Direct Consolidation Loan* is disbursed (paid out). Your first bill will be due approximately 2 months after the Direct Consolidation Loan is disbursed.

Chapter 4

Banking Basics

Financial Institutions

Financial institution can be considered pass-through organizations. When borrowers need funds, they must be linked with savers who provide the funds. Instead of borrowers, savers and lenders meeting at a designated location these needed funds are provided by financial institutions. Individuals as a group are the **net suppliers** for financial institutions because they save more money than they borrow. Firms also deposit some of their funds in financial institutions, primarily in checking accounts with various commercial banks. Like individuals, firms also borrow funds from these institutions, but firms are **net demanders** of funds because they borrow more money than they save. Financial institutions are necessary to provide a more efficient and effective method of exchanging financial resources. We learned in economics that markets exist because they provide a level of efficiency that would not otherwise exists. Without organized markets there would-be large-scale market inefficiency and corruption. Financial institutions practice a process of **financial intermediation**. Financial intuitions serve as intermediaries between lenders and borrowers, savers and investors, creditors and debtors.

Financial intermediaries offer economies of scale, liquidity and safety. Since financial intermediaries carry-out many transactions the cost per transaction is lower. Demanders of funds have many options to obtain their funds. People do not have to hide their money under their mattress to achieve a "state of liquidity". Individuals can write checks, make withdrawals at a physical location or Automated Teller Machine (ATM). Since funds kept in a financial institution are insured up to $250,000 by the *Federal Deposit Insurance Corporation* (FDIC), there is added safety provided by a financial instruction. There are a few major financial institutions that will be discussed. The financial institutions included in the following section are commercial banks, savings and loans, credit unions, pension funds, life insurance companies, mutual funds, hedge funds, trust companies and investment banks.

Commercial Bank: A commercial bank is a financial institution that provides its customers services to include lending, deposits, consumer loans, saving and checking accounts and certificates of deposits. Some commercial banks have physical locations, while others are completely online. Commercial banks make their profits by taking small, short-term, relatively liquid deposits and transforming these into larger, longer maturity loans. This process of asset transformation generates net income for the commercial bank. Note that many commercial banks do investment banking business although the latter is not considered the main business area.

Savings and Loan Associations: Savings and loans associations are depository institutions that receive their funds from savings and checkable deposits. Savings and Loans associations are known primarily for mortgage lending but this is changing. In the past they were regulated heavily, but due to the loosening of controls they perform many of the functions of a commercial bank.

Credit Unions: Credit unions, called by various names around the world, are **member-owned, not-for-profit financial cooperatives** that provide savings, credit and other financial services to their members. Credit union membership is based on a common bond, a linkage shared by savers and borrowers who belong to a specific community, organization, religion or place of employment. Credit unions pool their members' savings deposits and shares to finance their own loan portfolios rather than rely on outside capital. Members benefit from higher returns on savings, lower rates on loans and fewer fees on average.

Pension Funds: Pension funds are established by employers to assist their employees in saving for retirement. The collections of assets are invested in a way to provide stable and reliable growth for the long term. The income generated is meant to provide financial security to employees when they reach the age of retirement. Pension funds are the largest institutional investors in many nations. Institutional investors are groups with large amounts of capital to invest. Employers usually invest fixed contributions into a pension fund account, tax deferred, over a long period of time. **Life Insurance Companies:** Financial intermediary (the insurer) that shares the financial risk of untimely death of its policy holder (the insured). Life insurance companies insure individuals against pure risk. Pure risk is risk where there is a chance of a loss or no-loss. There is no chance for a gain. Life insurance companies ensure individuals for financial loss that occurs when an individual die. Life insurance companies also write annuities to provide future streams of income in the case of an untimely death of the supporting family member.

Mutual Funds: A mutual fund is an open-end investment company that raises money by pooling together the money of many investors. Pooling the money gives the fund the opportunity to purchase a large amount of shares. Investors benefit because they can own parts of companies that they could not afford to own alone. An open-end fund always issues new; redeemable shares, while a closed-end fund shares are limited. A closed-end fund is different from a mutual fund because there are a set number of non-redeemable shares offered. Mutual funds offer a variety of investment opportunities based on the investment objective. There are over 8000 mutual funds and they range from fixed income funds/bond funds to international funds. The underlying logic of mutual funds is that they provide diverse investments in stocks, bonds and cash without requiring investors to make separate purchases and trades. An individual would need more than $100,000 to build a similarly diversified portfolio of individual stock shares and bonds, but a mutual fund investor can send $1,000 to a fund company and find herself holding an ownership stake in a number of companies by purchasing a proportional share of the fund.

Hedge Funds: A hedge fund is an alternative investment vehicle available only to sophisticated investors, such as institutions and individuals with significant assets. Like mutual funds, hedge funds are pools of underlying securities. Also, like mutual funds, they can invest in many types of securities—but there are a number of differences between these two investment vehicles. Hedge funds raise money by offering institutional investors or high net worth individuals the opportunity to invest in more risky types of investments. Hedge funds are not highly regulated because of the perceived expertise of the investors. Hedge funds experienced both large losses and large gains from 1990s to 2008 due to the housing and financial crisis. However, according to Value Walk there were an additional 5,000 funds launched by the end of 2014. Finally, hedge fund managers are typically compensated differently from mutual fund managers. Mutual fund managers are paid fees regardless of their funds' performance. Hedge fund managers, in contrast, receive a percentage of the returns they earn for investors, in addition to earning a "management fee", typically in the range of 1% to 4% of the net asset value of the fund.

Trust Company: A trust company is a legal entity that acts as fiduciary, agent or trustee on behalf of a person or business entity for the purpose of administration, management and the eventual transfer of assets to a beneficiary. The entity acts as a custodian for trusts, estates, custodial arrangements, asset management, stock transfer, beneficial ownership registration and other related arrangements. A trust company does not own the assets its customers assign to its management, but it may assume some legal obligation to take care of assets on behalf of other parties. A trust company or trust department is usually a division or an associated company of a commercial bank. Trust companies often offer investment management and estate planning services.

Investment Bank: Investment banks assist corporations in issuing securities. Investment banks do not function like a commercial bank. Investment banks do not accept deposits or traditional loans. Investment banks advise corporation in securities issues pertaining to type of security and amount. Investment banks purchase shares from the issuing corporation and then sell them to the public in an **Initial Public Officering (IPO).** The two main lines of business in investment banking are called the sell side and the buy side. The "sell side" involves trading securities for cash or for other securities (e.g. facilitating transactions, market-making), or the promotion of securities (e.g. underwriting, research, etc.). The "buy side" involves the provision of advice to institutions that buy investment services. Private equity funds mutual funds, life insurance companies, unit investment trusts, and hedge funds are the most common types of buy-side entities.

Banks

A bank is a business. Banks sell services - financial services such as car loans, home mortgage loans, business loans, checking accounts, savings accounts, certificates of deposit, and credit card services. Some people go to the bank in search of a safe place to keep their money. Others go to the bank seeking money for loans to buy houses or cars, start businesses, expand farms, or do any of the other things that require borrowing money. Banks are able to lend money because they get it from all the people who open savings and other types of accounts. Banks act as an intermediary between the people who save and people who need to borrow. If savers didn't put their money in banks, the banks would have little or no money to lend. Your savings are combined with everyone else's savings to form a big pool of money. The bank uses that pool of money to make loans. The money doesn't belong to the bank's president, board of directors, or stockholders. It belongs to the depositors. That's why banks have a special obligation not to take big risks when they make loans. The money that you put into a bank account is safe. This may be the most important thing to understand about banks. If you put money under your mattress it can be stolen; if you put it in a jar it can be lost or it can burn in a fire. Bank accounts are insured by the FDIC, and credit union accounts by the NCUA, up to $250,000 per depositor in the case of bank failure (otherwise, there is no risk)

One thing to be mindful of, especially in your search for a bank, is that in most cases you do pay for the convenience of a bank account. Banks do tend to pay lower interest rates on interest-bearing accounts than do most brokerages and mutual fund companies that offer the same check writing privileges largely because of the guarantees associated with them. Also, very important to keep in mind is that banks usually tend to use different methods to calculate the interest rates they pay. To compare the rate and how much money you will earn from the various accounts, you need to ask for the "annual percentage yield." Banks will tend to quote both interest rates and the Annual Percentage Yield (APY), but keep in mind that the APYs are calculated the same everywhere.

The **Truth in Lending Act (TILA)** protects you against inaccurate and unfair credit billing and credit card practices. It requires lenders to provide you with loan cost information so that you can comparison shop for certain types of loans. For loans covered under TILA, you have a right of rescission, which allows you three days to reconsider your decision and back out of the loan process without losing any money. This right helps protect you against high-pressure sales tactics used by unscrupulous lenders. TILA does not tell banks how much interest they may charge or whether they must grant a consumer loan.

Choosing a Bank

Many banks offer similar services but as an informed consumer you can still make a distinction. You should consider available services, relationship accounts, future needs, and location. Are there specific services that are important to you, like online or phone access? If so, look for a full-service bank that offers a wide range of services, and make sure you're aware of any fees that may apply. Will you have more than one account with the bank (including a savings account or loan)? If so, look for an account that offers relationship benefits like higher interest rates on deposits or discounts on loan rates. If you're planning to buy a car in the next few years and will need a loan, evaluate the bank's loan programs as well as its checking and savings accounts.

Choose a bank that can support you as you grow. Is the bank convenient to where you live, work or go to school? Are there several branch and ATM locations? It can be expensive to use an ATM at another bank, because it may charge non-customers to use the ATM. Many regional banks, credit unions, and Internet banks offer free checking accounts, savings accounts, and access to ATMs. Consider that some institutions charge $35 for an overdraft, while others charge $10. Some make automatic loans to cover overdrafts, with APRs up to 36%. Some institutions can make an automatic withdrawal from your savings or charge to your credit card in the event of an overdraft, for no additional fee. Try to choose the least expensive option, given your spending habits. Sign up for text and/or email notification of large transactions and changes to your account information.

Types of Bank Accounts

Although banks offer a wide variety of accounts, they can be broadly divided into five types: checking accounts, savings accounts, certificates of deposit, money market accounts and individual retirement accounts (IRAs).

Checking account: A checking account offers easy access to your money for your daily transactional needs and helps keep your cash secure. Customers can use a debit card or checks to make purchases or pay bills. Accounts may have different options or packages to help waive certain monthly service fees. To determine the most economical choice, compare the benefits of different checking packages with the services you actually need.

What to consider in choosing a checking account:

- **Balance Requirements.** How much money must you deposit into your account when you open it, and how much must you keep in your account on a regular basis?
- **Fees.** Be aware of the fees that may be charged to your account. These may include fees for falling below a minimum balance, a monthly service fee, fees to order checks, fees for check writing or fees for specific transactions such as ATMs.
- **Interest.** Do you want to earn interest on your checking account balances? These accounts usually require a minimum opening balance and average balance during your statement period.
- **Other services** such as Online Banking and Bill Pay let you check balances and pay bills online. There might be a fee for Online Bill Pay.

Savings account: A savings account allows you to accumulate interest on funds you've saved for future needs. Interest rates can be compounded on a daily, weekly, monthly, or annual basis. Savings accounts vary by monthly service fees, interest rates, method used to calculate interest, and minimum opening deposit. Understanding the account's terms and benefits will allow for a more informed decision on the account best suited for your needs.

What to consider in choosing a savings account:

- **Interest rate.** What's the interest rate on deposits? Does the account pay a higher rate as your balance grows?
- **Balance requirements.** What amount is required to open the account? Can you avoid paying a service fee if you maintain a certain balance?
- **Fees.** What fees may be charged to your account?
- **Related accounts.** Will you be able to transfer funds easily between your savings and checking accounts?
- **Withdrawal limitations.** Will you be charged for making withdrawals over a certain number in a specific time period?

Certificate of Deposit (CD): Certificates of deposit, or CDs, allow you to invest your money at a set interest rate for a pre-set period of time. CDs often have higher interest rates than traditional savings accounts because the money you deposit is tied up for the life of the certificate – which can range from a few months to several years. Be sure you do not need to draw on those funds before you open a CD, as early withdrawals may have financial penalties.

Money Market account: Money Market accounts are similar to savings accounts, but they require you to maintain a higher balance to avoid a monthly fee. Where savings accounts usually have a fixed interest rate, these accounts have rates that vary regularly based on money markets. Money Market accounts can have tiered interest rates, providing more favorable rates based on higher balances. Some Money Market accounts also allow you to write checks against your funds, but on a more limited basis.

Individual Retirement Accounts (IRAs): IRAs, or individual retirement accounts, allow you to save independently for your retirement. These plans are useful if your employer doesn't offer retirement benefits or you want to save more than your employer-sponsored plan allows. These accounts come in two types: the traditional

IRA and Roth IRA. The Roth IRA is popular because the funds can be withdrawn tax-free in many situations. Others prefer traditional IRAs because these contributions are typically tax-deductible. Both accounts have contribution limits and other requirements you may need to discuss with your tax advisor before choosing your account.

Debit Card vs Credit Card

What Is a Debit Card?

Debit cards offer the convenience of a credit card but work in a different way. Debit cards draw money directly from your checking account when you make the purchase. They do this by placing a hold on the amount of the purchase. Then the merchant sends in the transaction to their bank and it is transferred to the merchant's account. It can take a few days for this to happen, and the hold may drop off before the transaction goes through. For this reason, it is important to keep a running balance of your checking account to make sure you do not accidentally overdraw your account. It is possible to do that with a debit card. You will have a PIN to use with your debit card at stores or ATMs.

What Is a Credit Card?

A credit card is a card that allows you to borrow money in small amounts at local merchants or online. You use the card to make your basic transactions. The credit card company then charges you interest on your purchases, though there is generally a grace period of approximately thirty days before interest is charged if you do not carry your balance over from month to month.

In the past many people felt that you needed a credit card to complete certain transactions such as rent a car or to purchase items online. They also felt that it was safer and easier to travel with a credit card rather than carrying cash or trying to use your checkbook. However, debit cards offer the same convenience without making you borrow the money to complete the transactions. It can be difficult to determine when to use a credit card or a debit card. It is better to use your debit card whenever possible, because it will prevent you from accidentally falling into the "credit card trap". When you can pay cash for most items, you are doing better financially. Some rental car agencies and hotels may still request a credit card over a debit card because they want to have a card where they can bill you for damages to their property. Be sure to check with the hotel or agency before you travel to make sure you can use your debit card instead of your credit card.

Chapter 5

Investing

Simply stated – investing means putting your money to work for you. There are many types of investments, and each client's goals and characteristics are unique – so each investment plan must take many factors into account. There is also a high emotional aspect to investing. Seeing losses – even if only "on paper" – can create strong feelings and inspire impulsive reactions. It's important for you to help your clients to better understand the potential implications of their investing decisions (and the potential impact of their emotions), as well as how to manage those decisions in order to meet their objectives.

This lesson will cover the following basic principles of investing:

- The Time Value of Money
- Suitability
  - Behavioral Finance: Risk vs. Reward
  - Risk Tolerance vs. Risk Capacity
- Pros and Cons of Pooled Securities

TIME VALUE OF MONEY

Many decisions in personal finance involve comparing the value of money at different points in time. The concept of the "Time Value of Money" refers to the idea that money available at the present time is worth more than the same amount of money in the future -- due to its potential earning capacity.

Here's a simple TVM example:

If you had $1,000 today and could earn 5% on your money in one year, you would have $1,050 a year from now. On the contrary, if someone offered to give you $1,000 one year from today, that gift would be worth only $952.40 right now (assuming the same 5% interest rate).

Let's look at a few other examples where you would use Time Value of Money to help make a financial decision:

You invest $1,000 today in an investment vehicle that promises to pay you back $1,500 in five years. Is this a good investment compared to a different investment that promises to pay you back $5,000 in 20 years?

A. I would choose $1,500 in five years.
B. I would choose $5,000 in 20 years.

Correct Answer: B.

In scenario 1, you would earn $500 over a 5-year period (or an average of $100/year). In scenario 2, you would earn $4,000 over 20 years (or an average of $200/year). Now a deciding factor could be how soon you needed access to your principal, but if that is not factored in, scenario 2 appears to be a more favorable deal.

You are considering two 5-year life insurance policies with the same death benefit. The first policy charges you a flat premium of $500/year for 5-years. The second policy charges you a $400 premium for the first year and then increases the premium by $60/year for each of the remaining four years. Which policy would cost you less?

A. The first policy
B. The second policy

Correct Answer: A.

Let's see if we can interpret this logically. In Policy 1, you would have paid $2,500 into the policy by the end of year 5. In Policy 2, you would have paid $2,600 ($400+$460+$520+$580+$640) into the policy by the end of year 5. All else being equal, scenario 1 appears to be the more favorable option.

You are looking at two apartments for rent. The first charges a flat rate of $900/month for a 3-year lease. The second charges $850/month for a 1-year lease. If you expect the rate to increase by 6% at the end of each of the next two years, which lease is the better deal over the 3-year period?

A. Apartment 1
B. Apartment 2

Correct Answer: A.

Apartment 1 seems straight-forward because you would pay $32,400 (or $10,800/year). Apartment 2 requires a little thinking. Since the interest is charged annually, we can look at the payment on an annual basis also, instead of a monthly basis. Consequently, the $10,200 paid annually would increase by 6% each year, so the year 2 payment would be $10,812 and the year 3 payment would be $11,461 for a total payment o $32,473. It appears that Scenario 1 is the more favorable option.

Basically - any time you have to compare the value of money at two different points in time, you are working a time value of money problem.

<u>TVM Equation</u>

In order to find the Present Value of a future sum of money, you would use the following equation: $PV = FV / (1 + i)^n$,

Where PV=Present Value, FV=Future Value, i=interest earned in that period, n=number of periods

In order to find the Future Value of a present sum of money, you would use the following equation: $FV = PV \times (1 + i)^n$

Let's put these equations to work:

1. Dave puts $1,000 into a savings account that pays interest of 7 percent. He plans to leave the interest and principal in the account for

10 years. How much will he have in his account at the end of the 10-year period?

The answer to the problem is $1,967.15. It would be computed as $\$1{,}000 \times (1 + 0.07)^{10} = \$1{,}967.15$

2. Dave would like to have $1,000,000 on the day he retires. He plans to retire in 30 years and believes he can earn a 10 percent rate of return on his money. How much would he have to set aside today to achieve his goal?

The answer to the problem is $57,308.55. This would be computed as $\$1{,}000{,}000 \times [\ 1 / (1 + 0.10)^{30}\ ] = \$57{,}308.55$

SUITABILITY

Definition: An investment selection process that ensures that the chosen strategy meets the goals, objectives, time horizon and risk tolerance of the investor.

Few things will derail your career faster than making unsuitable recommendations to a client. While there are a number of components which are viewed in the suitability category, three items that are significantly weighted are whether the recommendation met the client's Objective, Time Horizon, and Risk Tolerance.

Let's consider 3 scenarios where we consider a client's objective:

Scenario A: A client with a low income inherits some farm property. Since they don't know anything about farming, they decide to sell the property for $400,000 and invest the money with you for their retirement. You, in your desire to make them rich, invest the money aggressively. At the time that they are ready to retire, the market takes a turn for the worse, reducing their nest egg to $150,000.

How would you describe this client's likely objective?

A. Preservation of Capital
B. Income

C. Growth

Correct Answer: A This client's low income means they likely can't afford to lose their initial investment.

What might be ideal investments for this client?

A. Treasuries, Money Market instruments, or even a savings account.
B. Preferred Stock, Bonds/Bond funds or Dividend paying stocks
C. Growth/Aggressive Growth mutual fund or even individual stocks layers with options

Correct Answer: A. While typically providing a lower Return on Investment, these investment choices provide safety of principal.

Scenario B: A 78-year-old client becomes a widow. The insurance proceeds left by her deceased husband are critical to supplementing her pension and social security income.

How would you describe this client's likely objective?

A. Preservation of Capital
B. Income
C. Growth

Correct Answer: B. She needs the investment to spin off income.

What might be ideal investments for this client?

A. Treasuries, Money Market instruments, or even a savings account.
B. Preferred Stock, Bonds/Bond funds or Dividend paying stocks
C. Growth/Aggressive Growth mutual fund or even individual stocks layers with options

Correct Answer: B. These investment choices will generate potential income.

Scenario C: A 25-year-old client comes to you to invest $2,000/month so that she can retire at age 40. After receiving her MBA, she has recently received a job offer for $80,000 and she will continue living at home with her parents.

How would you describe this client's likely objective?

A. Preservation of Capital
B. Income
C. Growth

Correct Answer: C. She has a long, time horizon and wants to grow her investment significantly.

What might be ideal investments for this client?

A. Treasuries, Money Market instruments, or even a savings account.
B. Preferred Stock, Bonds/Bond funds or Dividend paying stocks
C. Growth/Aggressive Growth mutual fund or even individual stocks layers with options

Correct Answer: C. She is seeking a substantial return on her investment.

A client's Time Horizon can be short-term or long-term, so it is important that the product recommendation reflect the client's timeframe on use of the funds.

As an example, a client putting aside money for the down payment on a home would not need to have their money in an annuity product. Likewise, a client who doesn't need access to their funds for the next 40 years may not want to have their money sitting in a money market account.

With respect to Risk Tolerance, a client is either risk seeking or risk averse. However, clients tend to be more risk averse than they believe. When faced with a scenario of gain versus loss, most clients would settle for a limited gain if faced with a chance for a significant loss.

Behavioral Finance: RISK VERSUS REWARD

In the context of behavioral finance, "framing" is a cognitive bias where decisions are affected by facts or options presented (or "framed") as loss versus gain. Individuals will reverse their preference when a choice is presented as loss versus gain. The outcome of the decision can change based entirely on how the choice is presented. This is different from the traditional, rational approach, which would predict that the "frame" would have no weight on a decision.

For example – when the following gain/loss scenarios were presented with alternate frames, the resulting preferences were distinctly different.

Decision 1

- Option 1: Gain $240
- Option 2: 25% chance of gaining $1000 and 75% chance of gaining nothing

84% choose option 1 – even though the probability calculation should favor option 2:

100% * $240 = $240

25% * $1000 = $250

Decision 2

- Option 3: Lose $750
- Option 4: 75% chance of losing $1000 and 25% chance of losing nothing

When faced with this decision, there is an 87% preference of Option 4.

We see that when presented with a sure gain frame, the decision maker's preferred choice is risk-adverse (Decision 1). When the decision frame i loss oriented, the decision maker becomes more risk seeking (Decision 2).

Gain versus loss framing can also affect the way people look at additional financial resources. If an individual receives an additional $1,000 from a salary increase, it is seen in a gain frame, resulting in risk aversion. An individual who receives an additional $1,000 of spendable income from a reduction in taxes, sees the $1,000 in a loss frame, which results in risk seeking. The person who receives the salary increase (gain frame – risk avoidance) is less likely to invest than the person who receives the tax reduction (loss frame – risk seeking).

So how do you apply this to working with clients?

Advisors should attempt to present choices in a way to minimize the framing effect. Be aware of the potential of swaying a prospect or client's decision due to the way the advisor presents choices. Demonstrating a neutral option or framing the choice both ways can help the client make a less biased decision.

RISK TOLERANCE VERSUS RISK CAPACITY

Understanding a clients' risk tolerance is important – but it is equally important to understand their capacity for risk.

Risk Tolerance may be defined as

A. The inability to tolerate risk
B. Having an aversion to risk
C. Having a propensity towards risk
D. The ability to ignore risk

Risk Capacity may be defined as

A. Having inadequate financial resources for the risk chosen
B. Having a high emotional capacity for accepting risk
C. Having adequate financial resources for the risk chosen
D. Having a low emotional capacity for accepting risk

Risk Tolerance measures an individual's ability to handle risk. Persons with a high risk-tolerance are normally risk-seekers and are considered to have a propensity towards risk. In the investment arena, persons who trade options are considered to have a high risk-tolerance.

Risk Capacity measures an individual's financial capacity to handle losse in their portfolio; consequently, a person with a high degree of financial resources is deemed to have a high capacity to take on financial risks.

As financial services professionals, we must understand our clients' leve of Risk Tolerance and Risk Capacity. If they are afraid of losing even a small amount of money, they are considered risk averse (the opposite of risk tolerant). If they are living paycheck-to-paycheck or have little savings to fall back on, their Risk Capacity is considered inadequate.

Which of the following clients would require the most conservative investing approach:

A. High degree of risk tolerance and high degree of risk capacity
B. Low degree of risk tolerance and high degree of risk capacity
C. High degree of risk tolerance and low degree of risk capacity
D. Low degree of risk tolerance and low degree of risk capacity

Correct Answer: D. A client who is afraid of losing any of their investment, and also has little savings/disposable income, requires an investment strategy with the smallest degree of risk possible.

When working with Charles and Wendy, you recommend a portfolio of investments that provides a moderate risk strategy – despite the fact tha their Risk Profile lists them as highly aggressive. What other informatio might suggest that your recommendation would be suitable?

A. Your clients have little to no savings and minimal disposable income.
B. You personally tend toward a more conservative approach, so you advise your clients accordingly.
C. Your clients' time horizon is short-term.
D. A and C

E. None of the Above.

Correct Answer: D. Even though your client has a high tolerance for risk, if they also have a low capacity for risk, it should be factored into their strategy. Additionally, if they have a shorter time horizon, a less aggressive approach may be appropriate, as they would have less time to overcome potential losses.

PROS AND CONS OF POOLED SECURITIES

Individual Securities include all of the following investment items EXCEPT:

A. Common Stocks
B. Corporate Bonds
C. <u>Certificates of Deposits</u>
D. Treasury Bills

Correct Answer: C
Stocks, bonds and T-bills are all individual securities whose value will fluctuate based on market conditions and/or interest rates. A CD, in contrast, is similar to a savings account – it is insured (to FDIC limits) and is considered virtually risk-free.

Pooled Securities include all of the following investment items EXCEPT:

A. Unit Investment Trusts
B. Mutual Funds
C. <u>Certificates of Deposits</u>
D. Face Amount Certificates

Correct Answer: C
UITs, Mutual Funds and Face Amount Certificates are all examples of pooled securities because multiple investors purchase shares of the investments held within each. A CD is a bank deposit with a specified fixed term and interest rate.

An alternative to the direct purchase of stocks, bonds, and money market instruments is the purchase of shares in pooled securities (also known as an investment company). An investment company is an entity in which multiple investors pool their cash and then use this cash to buy securities. The investors own shares that are claims on the portfolio. Investment companies are structured in many different ways.

Pooled Securities (i.e. Mutual Funds, Unit Investment Trusts, REITS and Exchange Traded Funds) are often touted for their benefits (i.e. professional management, diversification, low minimum investment, etc.) as compared to individual securities.

Let's learn more about the four main types of Pooled Securities, and some of the advantages and disadvantages of each.

Mutual Funds

What makes mutual funds distinctly unique is that the only way an investor can buy shares in a mutual fund is from the fund itself through the creation of new shares. The only way an investor can sell shares of a mutual fund is back to the fund through the redemption (that is, liquidation) of shares. The great thing about mutual funds is that at least one (if not several) fund can match almost any objective or risk tolerance. Thus, when selecting a mutual fund for a client, the financial planner must ensure that the objective of the mutual fund matches the type of investment that is appropriate for the client, or at least that portion of the client's money. To facilitate this search, many organizations categorize mutual funds according to common objectives. Unfortunately, there is no universal categorization paradigm. So not only does a planner need to know what type of fund he or she is searching for, but which organization's classification scheme will produce the best grouping of funds for that search.

In general, mutual funds are classified by their Objective (i.e. growth, income, growth & income, etc.) or by their Underlying Investment (i.e. stock fund, bond fund, money market fund, etc.).

Benefits of Mutual Fund Ownership

Professional Management

Many investors lack the time and specialized knowledge needed to properly select securities and can better delegate this responsibility to others with more extensive education and access to information and resources.

Diversification

Small investors are effectively precluded from diversifying their portfolios

through the purchase of individual securities. They simply lack sufficient

assets to make reasonably sized purchases of a large number of assets.

In addition, the structure of transactions costs makes diversification more

expensive for small investors. Mutual fund portfolios typically include 50 to

200 securities, so buying even one mutual fund often means instant diversification.

Convenience

Most mutual funds offer services such as automatic reinvestment programs, check-writing privileges and electronic account transfers within the same fund family. In addition, they expedite record-keeping data such as account statements and tax information.

Other Factors

Additional factors that also encourage mutual fund ownership include:

• switching funds with minimal or no transaction fee.

• minimal investment requirements (most mutual funds have

minimum initial purchase requirements of under approx. $2,000.)

• regulation. (The recent scandals in the mutual fund industry notwithstanding, the extensive regulation of the industry by FINRA and the SEC should provide some comfort to investors.)

Drawbacks of Mutual Fund Ownership

- The major drawback to mutual fund ownership is the various fees and expenses.
- A more subtle drawback is that the investor loses control over the timing of capital gains.
    - When the fund manager declares a capital gain distribution, it triggers a taxable event for the owner of a taxable account.
    - Of course, the investor still has control over the timing o gains generated by the sale of the fund shares themselves.
- Another disadvantage, particularly for funds with large portfolios, is that mutual funds sometimes adversely affect the market prices of the stocks that they trade.

Real Estate Based Investment Companies

Mutual funds cannot own equity interests in real estate for several reasons, including the practical ones that daily price quotations are not available and there is a lack of marketability in the event of a large amount of redemptions.

Real estate investment trusts (REITs) are the most common vehicle for pooled investing in real estate. REITs assemble and manage portfolios of real estate and real estate loans. By law, at least 75 percent of REIT assets must be invested in real estate, and no less than 75 percent of income must be derived from real estate. In addition, to be recognized as a conduit and thus avoid taxation, REITs must pay out at least 90 percent of their income annually.

Advantages & Disadvantages:

Equity REITs are the most popular type with investors who want to participate in the growth of real estate values. Dividends should rise if rents increase more than expenses, and share prices generally reflect changes in property values. Mortgage REITs are similar to bonds. Like all interest-rate-sensitive investments, their prices rise when interest rates fall and fall when interest rates rise.

Unit Investment Trusts

There are two key features to a unit investment trust (UIT): The portfolios are unmanaged and they must have a termination date that is established at the time the UIT is created. The minimal management of these trusts means there are negligible management expenses. UITs are typically set up and marketed by a brokerage firm that receives an underwriting fee from the proceeds of the sale and manages the trust until it is liquidated. Investors technically buy units rather than shares.

Advantages and Disadvantages:

There are advantages and disadvantages to UITs, although many of these are similar to the advantages and disadvantages of other investment companies. The advantages are

- convenience.
- minimum investment size.
- portfolio stability.
- tax efficiency.
- negligible management fees.

The disadvantages are as follows:

- UITs are not as common as other forms of investment companies. Thus, an investor is less likely to find a UIT that seeks to fill a particular investment goal, especially with equity trusts.
- Front-end loads can be steep.
- The resale market is usually maintained by the trustee (the issuer). Such markets typically lack marketability and thus investors may have to sell their units at substantial discounts.

Exchange-Traded Funds (ETFs)

The portfolio of an ETF is typically, but not always, passively managed. Many are designed to mimic an index that reflects either the broad market, a sector, or an international index. ETFs do not sell individual shares directly to investors. Instead, they issue their shares in large blocks (blocks of 50,000 shares, for example) that are known as creation units. These units can only be bought with a basket of securities that mirrors the ETF's portfolio. Investors who want to sell their ETF shares can either sell them in the secondary market or, if they have enough shares to form a creation unit, exchange the creation unit for the basket of underlying securities.

Although we might think an investor would be indifferent between an index fund and an ETF, there are real advantages and disadvantages to each, and the financial planner should make sure that a client is being placed into the correct vehicle when one of these two investments is selected.

So - when should an advisor recommend an ETF, and when should he or she recommend an index fund?

If the client (or the planner) wants to engage in market timing trades, then index funds are generally preferable. Timing involves frequent trades. Although index funds can be bought or redeemed only at the end of the day, the transaction is often cost free. The commissions and bid-ask spreads make ETFs less appealing for this strategy. Conversely, investors with long-term objectives should prefer ETFs because the low annual expenses of managing the fund often easily offset commissions over a period of several years.

SUMMARY

Having a basic understanding of the following investing principles will help ensure you are making appropriate recommendations for your clients.

- Help your clients understand basic investing concepts, such as the time value of money.
- Discuss objectives, time horizon and risk tolerance to ensure you are making suitable investment recommendations.
- Be sure to consider how investment choices are presented or "framed," as this can significantly impact how a client perceives their choice.
- Remember that both risk *tolerance* and risk *capacity* are equally important factors in designing an investment strategy.
- Understand the advantages and disadvantages of the various types of pooled securities can help you make the most appropriate product recommendations.

Chapter 6
Asset Protection
(Insurance)

An old cliché reminds us that we need to build a house from the bottom up; so it is in financial planning. The Financial Planning Pyramid (see example below) is useful in providing a visual representation of the need to prioritize asset protection over asset accumulation. At the base of the pyramid are the items that ensure that the client can maintain their standard of living in the event of catastrophic losses (i.e. death, fire, loss of job, etc.). As we ascend the pyramid, we encounter items that provide for asset stability, and at the top we find items that, although risky, provide for asset growth.

A good financial advisor helps their clients protect the assets that they've worked so hard to accumulate. Most clients can easily understand the need to protect a tangible asset such as a car or home. However, an extended illness or injury, or a premature death, can be even more financially devastating than the loss of property.

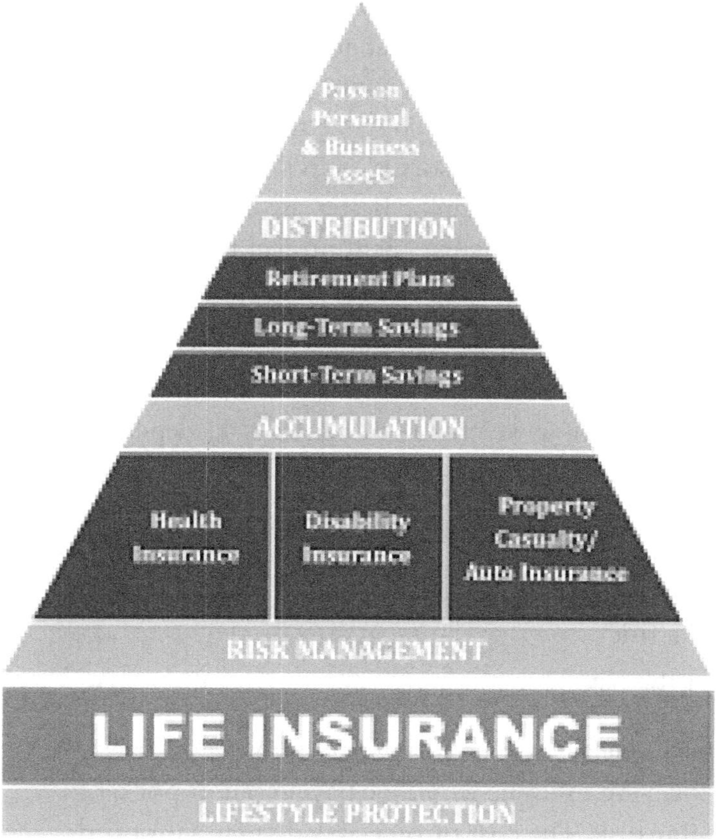

Image Source: Johnson Insurance: https://www.johnsoninsurancebp.com/

This module covers:

- Insurance as an Economic Tool
- Disability Insurance
- Life Insurance (Term vs. Permanent)
- Savings accounts, Money market accounts, CDs
- Mutual Funds, ETFs, Index Funds
- Stocks, Bonds
- Real Estate

INSURANCE AS AN ECONOMIC TOOL

Economics is predicated on human decision-making processes. Theory suggests that humans make decisions that are in their own best interest and are consistent in their preferences; consequently, consumers don't intentionally make decisions that would make them worse off. In most instances, consumers seek out advisors to help them accumulate assets for building wealth, so that they can be better off financially. However, part of an advisor's job is helping the client protect the wealth that they have built; this too makes them better off financially, but is seldom communicated that way.

Helping to protect a client from the financial risks that they face is an advisor's job; however, how we choose to handle risks depends on the situation. When it comes to dealing with risks, we have 4 options:

- Retain the risk
- Reduce the risk
- Avoid the risk
- Transfer the risk

An individual will typically retain a risk when both the severity and frequency are low. An example would be paying out of pocket to replace a Blue-Ray disk. The cost of Blue-Ray disks has dropped significantly and the need to replace if damaged is minimal. An individual would typically reduce a risk when both the severity and frequency are high. An example would be wearing a seatbelt while driving. Auto accidents happen every day and the results can be severe if one does occur. Rarely do we have the opportunity to avoid a risk. Once we leave the house for the day, we run the risk of any number of things occurring. An individual would typically transfer a risk if the severity is high and the frequency is low. An example would be purchasing homeowner's insurance to protect against catastrophic incidents. Insurance is purchased in situations where a consumer wants to transfer the risk of incurring replacement costs from themselves to the insurance company. The cost of replacing a home is high, but the frequency of a fire is deemed to be low.

There are five main types of insurance:

Property/Casualty: Protects against property losses to a business, home or car and against the liability that may result from injury or damage to others.

Health: Pays for covered medical expenses.

Disability: Replaces a portion of your salary if you are unable to work due for a period of time due to illness or injury.

Long-Term Care: Helps to pay for services such as assisted living facilities, home health care and/or nursing home stays.

Life: Protects a family or business from loss of income due to premature death

The commonality among all types of insurance is that they are designed to transfer risk and to protect income and/or assets. This section focuses on the two types of insurance designed to protect our greatest asset – our ability to earn an income: Disability Insurance and Life Insurance.

DISABILITY INSURANCE

Have you ever known anyone who has been disabled and out of work for a prolonged period of time? How did they meet their expenses? Many people have not considered the possibility that they may suffer a disabling injury or illness that prevents them from working nor the damaging effects a prolonged disability can have on their household's financial well-being. As a result, they either do not have disability coverage or have an inadequate amount of it. Income is the fuel of a household's financial engine. Without income, a household's economy will grind to a halt. Thus, the importance of protecting a client household from the loss of income due to a disability should be a high priority.

Disability income insurance is intended to replace lost earnings due to disability, as defined by the policy. Choosing a disability policy requires you to consider the following parameters:

1. when coverage is triggered

2. when benefits begin
3. how much is paid
4. when coverage ends
5. what the terms of renewing the policy are
6. what is not covered
7. what additional benefits and riders are available
8. how DI insurance is taxed

LIFE INSURANCE

Life insurance is perhaps rarely thought of as an "economic tool" but, the reality is that when structured properly, it can provide for cash accumulation, protect the family from depletion of their assets, and provide for the transfer of accumulated assets to future generations. What rational individual wouldn't choose to have insurance if it was presented in this light?

Although there are countless variations of life insurance policies available, once you understand the two basic types, you will learn that most everything else is a version thereof.

Term Insurance

Term Insurance is characterized by its "pure death protection", limited coverage window, and its options for renewability.

Term insurance consists of various types. Some with long durations and others much shorter (e.g. 20-yr versus 1-yr). It can be categorized by the premium payment (e.g. level-premium or decreasing-premium), the death benefit (e.g. increasing or decreasing), or the special benefits that may be available if the insured doesn't die during the term period (e.g. return of premium).

Permanent Insurance

Permanent life insurance is unique in that it offers permanent protection as long as the premiums are paid. While this permanent type of protection is in place, the policyholder has the opportunity for cash accumulation and/or policy loans.

Permanent life insurance can be divided into different categories (e.g. traditional and variable); however, this lesson features the traditional type (e.g. whole life, limited-pay life, and endowment). A key aspect of traditional permanent life insurance is that the product is based on guarantees: guaranteed premiums, guaranteed cash values and guaranteed death benefits. These elements seem to have resounded with the public after the economic uncertainty brought about by the great recession.

TERM VERSUS PERMANENT INSURANCE (The Age-Old Debate)

Some of the arguments in favor of term insurance can be described as criticisms of cash value (permanent) life insurance. Most of the arguments can be consolidated into two points of view:

1. Permanent insurance overcharges the policyowner.

2. The accumulation and protection elements should be separated (aka "Buy Term and Invest the Difference")

The basis for the first claim is the fact that if a policyowner dies in the early years of the contract, premium outlay under the permanent level premium plan is considerably larger than it would have been under a term plan. According to the term advocates, the policyowner paid a larger premium than was necessary. Term advocates question whether it is wise for the insured to pay in advance for something he or she may never need or live to enjoy. They argue that it is better "to pay as you go and get what you pay for."

There is no question that insureds are far better off financially with term insurance if they can be sure they will die within a relatively short time. On the other hand, they are far worse off if they guess wrong and live to a ripe old age.

The second claim—that the savings and protection elements of the contract should be separated—is based on the proposition that an individual can invest his or her surplus funds more wisely and with a greater return than the life insurance company can. Those who believe this recommend that individuals buy term insurance and then place the difference between the term premium and the premium they would have paid for permanent insurance in a separate investment program. This is known as a "buy-term-and-invest-the-difference" strategy.

While conceptually, this point may be valid – it's the reality of human nature that truly negates this argument. Most people are not disciplined savers and so in actuality, they will "buy term and spend the difference." And even if you are disciplined enough to "save the difference" - you are still left with the challenges of temporary coverage. This does not mean that term coverage is inherently bad – it means that you need to understand and talk with your clients about its drawbacks, so that when you are recommending term coverage, it's because the client's situation and goals make it the right solution.

So which should it be?

The buyers of term insurance typically differ from the buyers of permanent insurance because of specific characteristics of the buyer and their financial circumstances. In general, term insurance buyers are younger and have less disposable cash flow.

Agents selling term insurance should be cognizant of its uses and limitations so that, through recommendation, the coverage is suitable for the client's situation. When a temporary need exists or cash flow is limited, term serves as a viable solution to managing risk. However, in accepting term insurance as a means to manage risk, clients must also understand the parameters in which benefits are to be paid (e.g. within the term period) and the limit on perks (e.g. no cash value build up) beyond the death benefit.

The bottom line:

Whether term or permanent is the better product can only be answered if we know when the insured will die. If you knew the answer to that question, you could design a policy that exactly meets that period. Since we do not know when the insured will die, we need the type of insurance that best meets our ability to pay premiums and meet our financial goals and needs, over our lifetimes, so that the policy will be in force when death occurs or the need for insurance protection ends.

Only about 4 percent or 5 percent of term policies result in death claims, because the great majority of term policies are not in force when death occurs. One reason for this is that term insurance coverage has often ended before people reach life expectancy. In many cases, this is intentional. While initially people intend to keep term policies in force, they often change their minds when situations change. This occurs especially after retirement. Term insurance premiums become increasingly higher, no cash reserves are accumulating, and an expiration day is approaching. The insured's only option is to convert if a need still exists, perhaps at a premium beyond what the insured can afford or wants to pay. Another reason that term policies do not mature as death claims is that they have been converted to permanent policies.

Which type of life insurance is guaranteed to be in force when a person dies?

A. Term
B. Permanent
C. Neither

Correct Answer: B
Because permanent life insurance does not "expire," it is the only type of coverage that can be guaranteed to be in force when an insured die.

It is most important to first determine the right AMOUNT of coverage, and then determine the right type of coverage based on the client's budget.

A. True

B. False

Correct Answer: A. In many cases, using a combination of permanent and term coverage can accomplish this objective.

Term insurance can be most appropriate for older clients with a lower budget for premiums.

A. True
B. False

Correct Answer: B Term insurance tends to be best suited for younger clients because it will provide a low cost option that can get the amount of coverage needed within the given budget.

DETERMINING THE NEED

Why have life insurance?

Ben Baldwin gets to the heart of this question in his book, The Complete Book of Insurance (Irwin Professional Publishing, 1996). Mr. Baldwin says to answer this question, a person needs to ask two more questions. The first is, "In the event of my death, will anyone experience an economic loss?" If the answer is yes, then the second question is, "Do I care?" If the person does not have anyone who will experience a financial loss at his or her death, or if he or she does not care that those people will experience an economic loss, then that person is not a prospect for life insurance.

A human life has an economic value only if some person(s) or organization depends upon or expects to receive some monetary benefit through that life.

It would be difficult, if not impossible, to prepare a list of all needs that might possibly arise after the death of an income producer. Family circumstances differ, and a list of needs that would be appropriate for one family might be quite unsuitable for another. Even within any particular family, the needs picture changes from time to time.

Establishing how much life insurance a person should have requires a detailed analysis of the person' life circumstances. There is no blanket formula to determine this. The best approach is to look at the present and future financial needs of the family, identified through some version of a financial needs analysis.

A plan should be developed that can satisfy the agreed-upon need within the family budget. Sometimes, a combination of permanent and term life insurance is required to accomplish this.

There are several ways to calculate the amount of life insurance needed, ranging from simple to complex. One method is not necessarily better than another.

The three (3) main methods used to determine life insurance needs are:

1. Multiple of Income
2. Human Life Value
3. Financial Needs Analysis

Method 1: Multiple of Income

This method is derived from a simple rule-of-thumb where we multiply the client's income by some factor (typically 10, 15 or 20). As an example, a client earning $50,000/year would need $500,000 in life insurance if we multiplied by a factor of 10. There is no definitive thyme or reason to the multiplier, but it is suggested that the agent consider the client's age when making the projection.

EXAMPLE

Angus Lewis is a married male, aged 35, with gross annual earnings of $40,000 (expected level to retirement). Using the Multiple of Income

Method and a factor of 15, Angus would need $600.000 of life insurance.

Elements of Human Life Value Method

The philosophy behind this method is to calculate how much income the client will potentially generate over his/her lifetime.

The calculation is as follows:

- Average annual earnings estimate
- Taxes, self-maintenance costs, life insurance premiums
- Remaining years in workforce before retirement
- Estimated interest rate applicable to future working years

EXAMPLE (continued)

Let's go back to Angus McDonald. Let's assume Angus has $20,000 available annually to support his family. Angus plans to retire at age 65. The assumed interest rate is 5 percent. Thirty years of $1 payments has a present value of $15.37 [FV=0; N=30 years; I=5%; PMT=$1; PV=?]. This essentially says that if you wanted to receive $1 payments for the next 30 years, what amount would you have to begin with given a growth rate of 5%. If you used 4%, the PV=$17.29 Applying the five-step procedure produces the following results:

1. The average annual future earnings are $40,000.

2. The portion of the average annual future earnings available to the family per year is $20,000.

3. The number of years to retirement is 30.

4. The assumed interest rate is 5 percent.

5. The present value of future earnings to the family is calculated as follows:

$40,000 — $20,000 = $20,000,

$20,000 x $15.37 = $307,400.

FINANCIAL NEEDS ANALYSIS

The financial needs analysis approach is a way to determine how much life insurance a person should carry by analyzing the needs his or her family and other dependents would experience if that individual died.

Financial Needs Analysis—Amount of Insurance Needed
Estimated economic value or amount needed to fund desires
Amounts already available (Social Security, investments, existing insurance and retirement benefits and so on)
Unfunded amount that can be made up with life insurance

EXAMPLE

Married male aged 35, spouse aged 30, children ages 2 and 5

Income needed first 2 years $ 1,700 per month
Income needed next 14 years $ 1,460 per month
Income thereafter for surviving spouse $ 971 per month
Assumed interest rate 4%
Cleanup fund
$20,000
Mortgage redemption fund
$80,000

Emergency fund
$30,000
Education fund for children
$160,000
Combined needs (rounding to nearest $100)
$584,800

Estimated amount needed to fund desires (e.g. cleanup fund, lifestyle maintenance, mortgage redemption fund, education needs, and emergency needs) could equal $584,800. Subtract the amounts already available (estimated at $100,000). Unfunded amount that can be made up with life insurance is $484,800.

We can now compare the monetary value of the above financial-needs approach with the human life approach computed earlier. For purposes of comparison, assume—as in the case of Angus Lewis—that the family head is a male aged 35, has gross annual earnings of $40,000, and devotes $20,000 per year to his family. Assume that he has a wife aged 30 and two children, ages 2 and 5, and that an income of $1,700 per month is to be provided during the first 2 years, $1,460 per month during the next 14 years, and $971 per month thereafter for the life of the surviving spouse.

The total increases when the cash needs (cleanup fund, mortgage redemption fund, educational needs, and emergency needs) are added. Even if no provision is made for the children's college education, a cleanup fund of $20,000, a mortgage redemption fund of $80,000, and an emergency fund of $30,000 will increase the total to $424,800. If $80,000 is provided to each of the children for a college education, the total income requirements reach $584,800.

In the Angus McDonald scenario, which of the three methods produces the highest and lowest amount of need, respectively?

A. Multiple of Income, Financial Needs Analysis
B. Multiple of Income, Human Life Value
C. Financial Needs Analysis, Human Life Value

Correct Answer: B
The Multiple of Income approach estimated the need to be highest - $600,000. The Financial Needs Analysis estimated the need to be approximately the same - $484,800. The human life value approach results in the lowest estimated need of $307,400.

It is safe to assume that an adequate amount of life insurance for a family of 4 is approximately $500,000.

A. True
B. False

Correct Answer: B
The amount of life insurance an individual needs depends on many factors and varies based on each family's circumstances.

A human life has an economic value only if some person(s) or organization depends upon or expects to receive some monetary benefit through that life.

A. True
B. False

Correct Answer: A

SUMMARY

You have an opportunity to add tremendous value to your clients by helping them understand why insurance is an important economic tool, along with the explaining the various types of insurance coverage. Having a conversation about both disability and life insurance – explaining their options and helping to calculate their needs – will distinguish you from other advisors. It demonstrates that you are not focused on products – but want to help them build a solid financial plan with a base of protection.

Chapter 7

Borrowing (Debt)

Most of us don't have the ability to pay cash for every purchase we make – and even if we did, there are times when it makes more financial sense to borrow the money.

Borrowing creates debt (an obligation to pay). Borrowing can be viewed as an effective financial planning strategy because, on the positive side, it allows the consumer to acquire more assets than they otherwise might be able to, based on their available cashflow – for example, larger purchases such as a car or a home. However, many clients are unaware of how to assess when and how much to borrow – so they rely on others to do so for them. In fact, the recent foreclosure crisis in the US can be largely attributed to the fact that consumers borrowed more than they could reasonably afford to pay back.

Although many financial advisors may not see a financial benefit in helping clients deal with this aspect of their lives, having a clear understanding of how to effectively manage debt can be an effective way of not only **adding value to your clients**, but more importantly, of helping to "**find dollars**" in their budget that can be used toward achieving their goals.

In this lesson, we'll cover 3 critical Borrowing topics:

1) Types of Debt – Revolving and Installment
2) Amortization
3) Credit Scores

Let's start by looking at a real-life scenario:

> Owen's take-home pay is $4,000 per month. His balance sheet includes:

Home $200,000 Mortgage
$175,000 (5.6% interest)
Car $ 25,000 Car Loan
$4,000 (0% interest)
Savings Acct. $ 12,000 Student Loan
$7,000 (3.8% interest)
Credit Card Debt
$11,000 (12% interest)
Net Worth = $40,000

He has not begun saving for retirement but is concerned about having too much debt. He just received a promotion at work, so he has a $400 per month budget surplus. Which of the following might make the most sense for Owen to consider?

a. Allocate the $400 to pay off the credit card debt first; once that is paid off, take the $400 plus the regular credit card payment and put it into a retirement savings plan.
b. Immediately apply all of the budget surplus to retirement savings. Use the savings account to pay off the credit card.
c. Split the budget surplus between extra credit card payments and retirement (i.e. $200 toward each).
d. Retirement savings will have to wait; Allocate some of the $400 to current spending so that no new charges are made on the credit card. Use the rest to pay off the car loan first since it has the lowest balance. Then, focus on paying down the credit card.

REVOLVING DEBT

This type of debt can be characterized as debt that can increase of decrease based on the actions of the consumer.

An example of a revolving debt item is a credit card. The consumer can charge up the balance or pay it down. Although there is generally a maximum spending limit and a minimum monthly payment, the consumer largely decides what balance they will carry. Revolving debt can play a positive or negative role in financial planning.

In practical terms, your client will need a credit card to rent a car, secure a hotel room, pay for make online purchases, etc.; however, the over-use of credit card debt can lead to financial ruin. If your client maintains a budget for planned expenses, it may be acceptable for them to utilize the credit card for convenience or to obtain frequent purchaser points, but if they are incurring additional debt on the credit card because they lack adequate cashflow, new problems can occur.

Side bar: Check out this article with six simple factors to consider when choosing a credit card:

http://www.creditcards.com/credit-card-news/help/6-consider-before-choosing-picking-credit-card-6000.php

INSTALLMENT DEBT

This type of debt can be characterized as debt paid through fixed monthly payments.

Some common examples of installment debt items are car loans, student loans, and home loans. The consumer pays a fixed payment over a specified period of time until the debt is paid off.

Although making extra payments can help pay the debt off sooner than scheduled, one misconception of this type of debt is that making extra payments provides the debtor an opportunity to miss a payment if needed. Since consistent payments are required, any missed payment can cause the loan to go into default.

Installment debt can also play a positive or negative role in financial planning. The positive impact is relatively the same as the revolving debt; however, in the case of a missed payment, the negative impact could not only result in default, but repossession of the item used as collateral (in the case of the car or house) and possible wage garnishment (in the case of the student loan). Did you actually hear me say "wage garnishment". Yes, you did. Most student loans are government-based and any form of default could result in wage garnishment. Note that, if the Government is the creditor, permission is not required for your wages to be garnished or your bank account to be seized.

In working with your client to assess the degree of debt optimal for their income and goals, be sure to understand the terms (i.e. required length of payment, potential pre-payment penalties, interest rate, etc.) of the contracts.

Example of Installment Debt:

Loan variables such as term and interest rate can make a significant difference in your outlay over time. Let's look at an example.

Ethan plans to borrow $32,000 to purchase a new car over a five-year term.

What would you expect the difference in monthly payment to be between a 4.06% annual interest rate and a 7.06% annual interest rate?

a. Approx. $20/month
b. Approx. $45/month
c. Approx. $100/month
d. There should be no difference in the payment.

Let's find out if you were right.

Borrowing $32,000 over 5 years at 7.06% requires a monthly payment of $634.54. At 4.06%, the payment drops to $590.20. So the difference in payment is approx.. $45 per month – or $2,700 over the life of the loan.

Let's assume we borrow $32,000 for five years at 7.05%. What if we pay $50 extra each month….how much earlier would you guess our loan could be paid off?

a. 4 months

b. 7 months
c. 1 year
d. Our payoff date would remain the same.

Let's find out.

Remember that our required monthly payment was $634.54. If we add $50 per month – paying $684.54 each month – our loan will be fully paid off in 4 years, 8 months – saving us 4 months of time and over $500 in interest paid.

AMORTIZATION

Amortization really refers to the reduction in the amount of principal owed that occurs with each payment in an installment loan. A loan amortization table shows the portion of each payment that is interest and the portion that is repayment of principal. This table is important for two reasons. First, it clarifies how much would be owed if a loan were paid off early. Second, because the interest portion of a loan payment may be tax deductible, it is essential to know how much interest is paid each year.

Here is a simple amortization table:

Time Period	PMT	Principal Paid	Interest Paid	Total Interest Paid	Remaining Balance
Jan-21	$1,284.11	$1,221.61	$62.50	$62.50	$13,778.39
Feb-21	$1,284.11	$1,226.70	$57.41	$119.91	$12,551.69
Mar-21	$1,284.11	$1,231.81	$52.30	$172.21	$11,319.87
Apr-21	$1,284.11	$1,236.95	$47.17	$219.37	$10,082.93
May-21	$1,284.11	$1,242.10	$42.01	$261.39	$8,840.83
Jun-21	$1,284.11	$1,247.28	$36.84	$298.22	$7,593.55

Jul-21	$1,284.11	$1,252.47	$31.64	$329.86	$6,341.08
Aug-21	$1,284.11	$1,257.69	$26.42	$356.28	$5,083.39
Sep-21	$1,284.11	$1,262.93	$21.18	$377.47	$3,820.46
Oct-21	$1,284.11	$1,268.19	$15.92	$393.38	$2,552.26
Nov-21	$1,284.11	$1,273.48	$10.63	$404.02	$1,278.78
Dec-21	$1,284.11	$1,278.78	$5.33	$409.35	$0.00

There are some strategies to debt reduction that are based on understanding amortization tables. Studies for paying off mortgage loans early have shown that one extra payment per year can knock 9 years off of a 30-year loan. Strategically, this can be done by making the extra payment any time during the year as a lump sum, or by splitting the regular monthly payment into 2 semi-monthly payments. In all practicality, the goal is to eliminate the additional interest being charged on the outstanding balance.

Other debt reduction strategies that have been effective for eliminating amortized loans are "Snow-Balling" and "Highest Interest". In the snow-balling approach, the goal is to assess which debt has the highest feasibility of being paid off first, then taking that payment that was being made and applying it to other debt. Theoretically, the monthly outlay remains the same, but the timeframe for reducing a specific debt increases exponentially. In the highest interest approach, the goal is to give the least amount of money away in the form of interest. By attacking the items with the highest effective interest, you essentially make additional payment towards principal, thereby saving money in the long-run because less money will be applied to interest.

Here is an example that combines these two strategies:

While it is a fact that these strategies work effectively towards amortized loans, they can be applied towards any type of debt.

CREDIT SCORING

Credit Scoring is a numerical method of representing a consumer's creditworthiness. A set of complex algorithms are used to analyze components of a consumer's credit file resulting in a specific number ranging from approximately 400-850. There are several agencies (e.g. EQUIFAX, Trans Union, and Experian) that utilize credit scoring models; consequently, the scores differ across agencies.

Credit scoring has become a way of life and the only way to ensure your success is to understand the rules of engagement. There are 5 components to the credit score (all of which the consumer has total control). Yes, the scoring models reflect your behavior and you can manipulate the models in your favor if you understand that you are in control.

Components of the Credit Score

- Payment History (35%)
- Debt Level (30%)
- Length of Credit History (15%)
- Inquiries (10%)
- Mix of Credit (10%)

Since the score associated with *Payment History* is based on whether you pay your bills on time, you have total control over that component. *Debt Level* is associated with the amount of debt owed compared to the amount of available credit you have. The circumstances are rare when you would need to max-out your available credit, so you can control this aspect as well. Think of it this way, when your credit card is full you stop charging because you have to, so why not stop voluntarily? *Length of Credit History* is comprised of all of the types of debt that you have based on the length of time those line items have been in place. Too often consumers close out their oldest card because it has a small limit (e.g. the one that they received while in college). If there is a 6 year difference between the card you acquired your freshman year of college and the one that you received after landing your first job, you've lost 6 years of history by closing out the first card. *Inquiries* are attempts to obtain credit. When the attempts are voluntary, the consumer is making a conscious effort to acquire new lines of credit. If this is done too often and credit is not granted, the score reflects negatively. The exception to this would be if you are applying for a mortgage or car loan where the loan is "shopped" around within a 30-day period. Sometimes the attempts are involuntary. In these instances, existing creditors may make periodic reviews of your accounts to make decisions as to raise or lower your limits. If you receive "pre-approved" offers, note that no inquiry has been made, but will result in an inquiry if you decide to apply for that offer. Be mindful that you have total control over the number of times that you apply for credit. *Mix of Credit* is determined by the relative number of revolving and installment accounts that you have. While carrying too much debt may not fare well in your favor, a good balance of lines of credit (with low balances) will. In theory, creditors monitor other creditors' interest in you; therefore, when you have a history of multiple lines of credit, you are viewed favorably.

A client with a high credit score has a better opportunity to leverage the credit available to them than one with a lower credit score. The lower interest rates, transaction costs, and payments associated with a high credit score create a unique opportunity for a client to utilize their available cash for asset building.

> Let's look back at an earlier example. Ethan wanted to borrow $32,000 to buy a car. Do you remember the difference between his monthly payment based on a 7.06% interest rate vs. a 4.06% interest rate? With a strong credit score, Ethan is more likely to secure the better rate of 4.06% -- and thus save himself $2700 over the life of his loan. Good credit pays off!

Summary

Now that we've learned a bit more about borrowing and debt, let's go back to Owen's scenario and see if we would change our recommendation.

Correct Answer – No matter which answer they choose, it should still say:

> Maybe?? The reality is that any of these might be the right solution for Owen – so the best way to help him would be to talk through the options and help him land on what makes the most financial sense and best addresses his objectives.

There are many ways to borrow money, and most clients you work with will have some sort of debt as part of their balance sheet. Understanding these basic principles of borrowing –

- The difference between revolving debt and installment debt
- The impact that the variables of borrowing – time period, interest – have on repayment
- How to amortize a loan, and how to use that information to make decisions about the best approach to paying off debts
- The impact of a credit score

-- will help you to ask the right questions to understand your client's financial situation and to add value by helping them make informed financial decisions when it comes to debt.

Chapter 8

Taxes and Your Paycheck

Tax Basics

Income in the United States is taxed by the federal government, most states governments and many local governments. The federal income tax system is progressive, so the rate of taxation increases as income increases. Marginal tax rates range from 10% to 37%. The federal personal income tax that is administered by the Internal Revenue Service (IRS) is the largest source of revenue for the U.S. federal government. Nearly all working Americans are required to file a tax return with the IRS each year and most pay taxes throughout the year in the form of payroll taxes that are withheld from their paychecks.

Many states as well as some cities and counties have their own income tax, which is collected in addition to the federal income tax. States that do have a state income tax require that you file a separate state tax return and have their own rules. If you are curious about a particular state's tax system and rules, visit one of your state's tax pages. If you've never filed taxes, it can seem pretty intimidating. However, before you file your taxes it is prudent to learn some basic terminology.

Below are some basic tax preparation terms:

Earned income – Salaries, wages, tips and professional fees, including taxable scholarships and fellowship grants. Earned income is the most taxed form of income. With personal tax rates ranging from 10% to 37%, this amount can easily add up. Earned income is also subject to other taxes as well, such as social security and Medicare taxes, which are 12.4% (half paid by employer) and 1.45%. Therefore, earned income can be taxed at almost a rate of 50%.

Unearned income – Investment-type income like interest on your savings account, dividends and capital gains, as well as unemployment compensation.

Gross income – All income you received in the form of money, goods, property and services that is not exempt from taxes.

Gross Income Inclusions

Gross income is generally the total amount of income received from all sources before exclusions and deductions. Gross income falls under four major types: active, passive, portfolio and other. The distinction between these types dictates the treatment used for losses. All of the following would be considered gross income.

Wages and tips	Taxable pensions and annuities
Self-employment tax	Rents
Taxable scholarships	Royalties
Taxable interest and dividend	Annuities and pensions
Capital gains	Trust distributions

Exclusions from Gross Income

Tax-exempt interest	Life Insurance proceeds
Tax-free fringe benefits	Reimbursement for business expenses
Qualifying scholarships	Worker's competition
Qualified Roth Distributions	Social Security

Exemptions – A predetermined amount of money you can deduct from your taxable income for basic living expenses. You, as an individual, may be an exemption, and dependent children (which you probably are to your parents) qualify as exemptions.

Standard deduction – A set amount of money that the federal government gives you if you meet certain stipulations. It differs according to marital status. Generally, a taxpayer can claim the standard deduction (fixed amount) or itemize their deductions (total your actual expenses on Schedule A) and subtract this amount from their adjusted gross income (AGI) to determine their taxable income.

Types of Standard Deductions
For taxpayers who elect not to itemize their deductions, a standard deduction amount is available for all taxpayers. For 2020, the standard deduction amounts are as follows:

Married Filing Joint Returns and Surviving Spouses - $24,800
Heads of Households - $18,650
Single Individuals (other than Surviving Spouses and Heads of Households) – $12,400
Married Filing Separate Returns – $12,400

For 2020, the standard deduction amount for an individual who may be claimed as a dependent by another taxpayer cannot exceed the greater of:

(1) $1,150 or
(2) the sum of $350 and the individual's earned income.

The additional standard deduction amount for the aged or the blind is $1,50. These amounts are increased by $1,300 if the individual is also unmarried and not a surviving spouse

Itemized deductions – There are six main categories of expenses that can be deducted: medical and dental, taxes, interest, charitable contributions, and casualty and theft losses. Itemized deductions reduce the amount of tax you owe.

Common itemized deductions:

- Medical expenses – In 2020, the IRS allows all taxpayers to deduct the total qualified unreimbursed medical care expenses for the year that exceeds 10% of their adjusted gross income.

- Mortgage interest expenses – Qualified residence interest (primary and one other residence)
- Charitable contributions – All public charitable contributions (up to 50% of AGI) and private foundation charitable contributions (up to 30% of AGI)
- Real estate taxes – State, local and foreign real estate taxes
- Casualty and theft losses – Identifiable event and/or property damage results, when event is sudden, unusual and unexpected.
- Investment interest – Limited to net investment income
- Miscellaneous expenses – Subject to 2% of AGI floor: job search costs, uniforms, professional dues,
- Personal property taxes – State and local personal property taxes
- hobby expanses, work tools, expenses to collect income. Not subject to 2% AGI floor: gambling losses, amortizable premium on taxable bonds, federal estate tax in respect to a decedent, unrecovered investment in annuity contract.

W-2 Forms – Wage-income forms that you receive from employers in order to prepare your taxes.

Filing status – Whether you are single, married or head of household. There are several sub-categories within each of these as well.

Single	A single filer is someone that was unmarried, separated or divorced at the end of the year
Married Filing Jointly	Taxpayers who are married at the end of the year can file married filing jointly. If your spouse died during the year, the survivor may still file MFJ for that year. As pf 2014, the IRS allows same-sex married couples to file jointly as long as they were married in a state that recognizes same-sex marriages
Married Filing Separately	If you are married, you can file MFJ or married filing separately. The amount of tax due is generally lower with MFJ, but some couples prefer to file separately to use thei own income, exemptions, deductions and credits.
Head of Household	Unmarried taxpayers who maintain a household for a qualifying person can file as head of household. To qualif for HH, the taxpayer must pay more than half the cost of maintaining a household for a qualified person (principal home).
Qualified Person	Child, grandchild, parents, grandparents, siblings, step child, adopted child, step-family members, in-laws and blood uncles, aunts, nieces and nephews.
Qualified Widow(er)	***with dependent child*** – A taxpayer can use this filing status for the two tax filing years after the death of their spouse if the taxpayer has a qualified dependent.

Depending on your gross income, you may or may not be required to file. For example, in 2019, all single individuals under 65 wit a minimum gross income of $12,200 were required to file. Even if your parents (or someone else) can claim you as a dependent, you may be required to file if you meet certain income conditions. When determining your income, be sure to include all taxable income you receive. If your scholarships are not taxable, you need not include them in your income. (Non-taxable scholarships carry no service requirement and are used to cover education-related expenses). But if your scholarship money is paid in exchange for teaching, research or other services, it is taxable – even if you don't receive a W-2. This includes work-study income and pay you receive as a teaching or residential assistant.

Choosing a Tax Filing Form

To file your taxes, you need to fill out one of three basic forms:

- **1040EZ:** The simplest tax form; consists of a single page. Requires a taxable income of less than $50,000 and interest income of less than $400. Restricted to singles and couples with no dependents. Cannot itemize deductions or deduct IRA contributions.
- **1040A:** A more complicated form, allows more flexibility in income sources (including pensions, IRA dividends and retirement benefits). Also requires a taxable income of less than $50,000. Cannot itemize deductions but can deduct IRA contributions.
- **1040:** The most complicated form, sometimes called the "long" form; required if income is more than $50,000. Can itemize deductions to adjust income.

For most students, the Form 1040EZ will suffice. If you're not sure and want to include more sources of income and deductions, you can always file one of the more complicated forms. If you itemize your deductions, you'll also have to complete Schedule A of your 1040.

Other common tax forms.

Form W-2: If you were employed and had taxes withheld from your paycheck, you receive Form W-2 at the end of the year for each of your jobs. It lists how much you were paid all year, how much was withheld in federal, state, and local taxes, and other information necessary to file. Note that all this information is also supplied to the IRS by each employer.

Form W-4: Each time you start a new job, you need to fill out Form W-4. It tells your employer how much to withhold in taxes from your paycheck, based on your number of qualified dependents and filing status. If you recently got married, divorced, had a baby, or had one leave the nest, update this form to reflect the change. That way, your employer won't withhold too little or too much.

Form 1098: There are multiple iterations of Form 1098, but all of them provide information on potential tax deductions. Mortgage interest, student loan interest, and tuition payments are common items reported on Form 1098. For instance, if you paid interest on a mortgage loan on your primary residence and also paid student loan interest, you should receive two separate 1098 forms reporting information pertinent to each.

Form 1099: This form reports a wide range of non-salary income. If you're an independent contractor, received interest or dividend payments, withdrew money from a retirement account, or had a debt canceled, you'll likely receive a 1099 reporting it. Self-employed earnings are reported on Form 1099-MISC.

Itemizing Deductions

The federal governments allows you to deduct certain specified expenses from gross income. The result is a lower tax base – and less tax that you have to pay. You'll need to fill out the 1040 if you want to itemize deductions.

You should itemize your deductions if they total more than your standard deduction (the standard amount you deduct from gross income on the 1040EZ and 1040A forms). However, certain people must itemize even if their deductions are less than the standard deduction. For example, you must itemize if you are married, but filing separately and your spouse is itemizing; or if you are a nonresident or dual-status alien.

When to Pay your Taxes

The deadline for taxes is April 15 after the year for which taxes will be filed. "You can get an automatic four-month extension. but this is not an extension for paying. It's only an extension to file. If you know you're going to owe taxes, you still have to pay by April 15.

Getting Help filing your Taxes

The IRS now has a 24-hour, 7-day toll-free number to help answer questions during the tax crunch period. The number is 1-800-829-1040. You can also call this number to get the location of the nearest IRS office. You can get free tax assistance at any IRS office. However you are encouraged to look for help online at www.irs.gov.

The IRS also has a few publications that can help you:

- IRS Publication 17: Your Federal Income Tax
- IRS Publication 970: Tax Benefits for Education

Learn the basics for how to file, and come next April, you can file your taxes with ease.

Passive Income

This type of income comes from activities in which you do not actively participate. Such activities include income from real estate and certain business arrangements, such as limited partnerships. Special rules regarding passive activity losses were enacted in 1986 to limit the amount you could reduce your tax liability from passive income. However, you can still reduce your non-passive income up to $25,000 if your income is below $150,000 and you actively participate in passive rental real estate activities. This amount is phased out between $100,000 and $150,000. Other than this exception, you may only claim losses up the amount of income from the activity. Losses that cannot be claimed are carried forward until the property is disposed of or there is adequate income to offset the loss. Real property and other types of investments, if they qualify, may also be used in a 1031 exchange to avoid paying taxes on the income from the sale of the property. This only applies if the proceeds from the sale are used to purchase a similar investment.

Taxes Rates

(for taxes due in April 2020, or in October 2020 with an extension)

Single	Married, filing jointly
$0 to $9,700	$0 to $19,400
$9,701 to $39,475	$19,401 to $78,950
$39,476 to $84,200	$78,951 to $168,400
$84,201 to $160,725	$168,401 to $321,450

Understanding your Paycheck

Most paychecks have two parts—your check stub and your paycheck.

A pay stub generally lists:

- Your taxable earnings
- Your gross pay or the total amount of money that you earned that pay period
- Your net pay or the amount of money that you get to take home with you. Your net pay matches the dollar amount listed on the paycheck that you're so eager to cash.
- Withholdings for federal taxes, state taxes, Social Security and Medicare, which largely account for the difference between your taxable earnings and net pay

Each pay stub includes year-to-date fields for each withholding category so you can track how much money you've paid for taxes and Social Security and Medicare throughout the year. Many employees include a similar listing for contributions to retirement savings plans and health plans. You'll generally see these fields marked as "YTD" (year-to-date) on your pay stubs. A pay stub also lists gross and net income to-date. So you're able to track just how much money you're making (your gross pay) and how much money you're actually taking home after taxes and other deductions (your net pay) throughout the year.

Approximately 31% of your paycheck is deducted for taxes with taxes paid immediately on earned income. Below are common paycheck deductions:

Fed Tax: I think this one is pretty simple. This is the federal tax you pay from each check.

State Tax: Again, a basic concept. This would be the state tax you pay. Usually you will not find a separate locality pay, but it does happen occasionally. Your locality is usually a city such as Baltimore City.

FICA: This is your social security tax. You pay 6.2% of your salary to FICA. It stands for Federal Insurance Contribution Act. Don't feel too bad though, because your employer contributes an additional 6.2% into FICA also, so really 12.4% of your salary goes into social security, but only half of that is actually pulled away from you.

Med: You have probably heard of Medicare. This is the system that helps the elderly with medical expenses. You pay 1.45% towards Medicare. Your employer matches the same amount.

Health: Your health insurance may be taken from your paycheck either pre-tax or post-tax. Either way it gets taken out of the gross amount and makes your net amount smaller. For most people, their employer actually pays a much larger share of the health insurance cost than they do.

Life: Your employer may offer a life insurance policy. The policy is usually for a small amount, such as two times your annual salary.

Retirement: There are several categories available here. This could be the amount you chose to contribute (such as a 401(k)), or perhaps your employer automatically deducts a certain percentage and places it into an account for you.

FSA: The Flexible Spending Account is an amount you choose to set aside for medical costs.

ESOP: The Employee Stock Ownership Plan is a benefit you signed up for. If you did not, go and speak to someone in your human resource department. The ESOP is money taken from your paycheck and used to purchase company stock. Sometimes the company will match a portion of your ESOP contribution, but they do not have to. An ESOP is another form of savings.

Voluntary Contributions: Your voluntary contributions consist of items you voluntarily sign up for, like health insurance, dental and vision insurance, and retirement plans.

Involuntary Items: Involuntary items are also withheld from your paycheck. These can include child support, defaulted student loans, taxes, and unpaid court fines.

Net Pay: This is what you get to take home, after all deductions.

Methods of Receiving Wages

You can receive you pay in the form of a **paycheck, payroll card**, and **direct deposit.** A paycheck is the most common method of payment from employers that shows taxes paid and other deductions.

Paper checks allow you to keep your bank account information private from your employer. With your paycheck in your hand, you have control over when your money is available to you. If you don't have a bank account, you never have to worry about getting hit with bank fees. If you don't want your spouse knowing how much you are earning, paper checks can help conceal that information. For example, if you have a joint account for direct deposit, the other account holder can see deposited amounts. Your paper check, however, is handed to you alone. Paper checks are susceptible to theft, loss and damage. Depending on the situation, your employer can charge you for having to replace a paper check. On a holiday or weekend, you may have to wait until the next business day to cash your check. If you are out sick or on vacation, you probably won't get your paycheck until you return to work. You have to make trips to the bank to cash or deposit your check, which results in lost time and money. Whether your employer can force you to accept direct deposit depends on state law. The state might allow it if you get to pick your own financial institution or your employer offers an alternative payment method, such as cash or paper check. In some states, employers must get employees' approval to use direct deposit.

Paper check is an acceptable method of payment regardless of where an employer is located, as long as it can be converted to cash.

Payroll cards are essentially prepaid debit cards that are loaded up by employers every pay period. The cards can make purchases at a point of sale and be used at ATMs to withdraw funds loaded on them. For businesses, the cards are part of a push to finally get rid of paper payroll checks, which are vulnerable to fraud and costly to print and get into the hands of employees. Businesses have been trying for years to push as many employees as possible into direct deposit. But in order to ditch paper paychecks altogether, banks have to find some way to pay employees who can't or don't want to have their paycheck direct-deposited into a checking account. One benefit of depositing your employee paychecks to a debit card is the fast delivery of funds. Submitting your payments electronically gives your employees quicker access to their funds. It is also a reliable method of delivering funds to all employees at the same time in the same manner, as some may not have a bank account for a standard payroll direct deposit. Providing payments directly through a debit card allows a business to save money on paper used to print checks. It also can save employees the effort and cost of cashing their checks at expensive check-cashing stores. With a debit card, they simply can withdraw the funds at an ATM or make a purchase and get cash back to access the funds. One other benefit of offering payroll debit cards to employees is that it allows the employee to better manage his money: Instead of withdrawing his entire paycheck, he can submit payments or withdraw cash a bit at a time.

As with a standard debit card, there is always the risk that an employee with lose her debit card. Some stores do not always check for identification when someone comes in to process a credit card transaction. In this case, if someone uses a stolen card and chooses to process his payment as a credit card, employer and employee lose that money. The employer has to work to recover those funds from the merchant via his payroll administration company, and the employee may have to wait days after payday to access his pay. The employee may have to pay ATM withdrawal fees when attempting to access his debit card funds. In some states, an employer must provide a fee-free way for the employee to receive his pay, so the employer would have to cover these ATM fees. For instance, in Texas, a withdrawal fee to the employee could conflict with the Texas Payday Law; as of 2010, there are no solid precedents to test the law in that situation. Additionally, some bank ATMS have a maximum withdrawal limit, so the employee could run into issues if he urgently wants to access his entire paycheck.

Direct deposit is safe, so you don't have to worry about stolen, damaged or lost checks. With direct deposit, you don't have to make trips to the bank to cash your check. If payday falls on a holiday or weekend, you may get your money early, on the prior business day. If you're off work on payday, you can still access your pay. Your money may be in your account on payday morning, regardless of what time your employer hands out paychecks. Direct deposit lets you make split deposits into multiple bank accounts to separate your savings from bill payments. One disadvantage of direct deposit it that you must give your employer your bank account information to receive direct deposit. If you don't qualify for a bank account, you can't get direct deposit. Some employers offer payment by payroll card to employees who can't get an account, but these often have fees attached. Another disadvantage of direct deposit is the possibility of getting slapped with bank charges if you fail to manage your funds properly.

Chapter 9

Retirement Planning

Retirement Needs Analysis

There are many factors to consider when trying to determine the funds needed to successfully retire. These factors include life expectancy, inflation, desired retirement lifestyle, and projected investment return.

Life Expectancy

Life expectancy - the age until which a person is expected to live - is a second critical factor in determining how much money an individual will need to set aside for retirement. Working longer will reduce the number of years in retirement and, therefore, reduce the level of assets needed to fund that retirement. **Joint Life Expectancy -** For couples, the average number of years until the second person's death is longer than the individual life expectancy of either person alone. This means using whichever person's life expectancy is greater will result in underestimating the retirement needs of a couple.

Inflation

The rate of inflation can have a huge effect on a retiree's standard of living, as it erodes the buying power of income that, in large part, may be fixed. Inflation occurs when day-to-day expenses rise. An imbalance in the relationship between supply and demand causes inflation. Prices rise as increasing numbers of people compete to buy a limited number of goods. Periods of inflation are common in functioning free market economies. However, inflation can have a profound effect on your standard of living. A realistic projection of future inflation rates is needed to calculate the income and assets needed to retire.

Desired Lifestyle in retirement

The type of lifestyle an individual or couple seeks to live in retirement will greatly affect the level of retirement assets and income needed. Factors to consider:

- Travel plans

- Housing
- Hobbies
- Entertainment

Project investment returns

The rate of return an investor will earn while saving for retirement and then in retirement also require assumptions about the unknown. To be on the safe side, many planners use conservative estimates that may be a couple percentage points below historic rates of return.

Retirement Income Sources

Employer-Sponsored Plans

The trend in employer-sponsored plans is away from defined benefit plans that guarantee a set benefit at retirement, depending on age, years of service and salary. The trend is toward defined contribution plans under which the employee contributes some, if not all, of what is being saved on their behalf. Among defined benefit pension plans, the most generous ones do not come close to replacing the income a worker earned while employed.

Social Security

Social Security benefits also are not intended to fully replace what a retiree earned while working. In considering retirement income, a critical question is when to begin collecting Social Security benefits. The longer an individual waits, the greater the monthly benefit will be.

Personal Savings

Savings outside of employer-sponsored retirement plans are another source of retirement funds. These funds may be in taxable accounts, and therefore the tax implications of selling these assets for use in retirement must be considered.

Other retirement income sources may include anticipated inheritances, dividends, real estate, gifts or bonuses.

- **Dividend: Equity income investments.** Designed to provide long-term growth and income, equity income investments can help offset the effects of inflation. But, because of their growth potential, they are also subject to market volatility. As you approach retirement, keeping a portion of your investable assets invested in high-quality, dividend-producing stocks and equity mutual funds can hedge your retirement portfolio from inflation risk. These investments also give your portfolio the opportunity to benefit from strong market performance — which is increasingly important for retirees, as many people are spending 20 or more years in retirement.

- **Interest: Bond and fixed income investments.** Interest-bearing investments offer the benefit of a stable, low-risk income stream, while also preserving your principal investment. They may offer protection against market volatility, but may also be subject to credit risk. As you near retirement, increasing your interest-bearing investments may help protect your portfolio from market fluctuations

Charitable and Beneficiary Gifting Goals

Wishes to make charitable gifts either in life or upon death should be taken into consideration when calculating financial needs for retirement. Lifetime charitable gifts will need to be built into a retirement cash flow plan. If an individual wishes to leave money to a charitable organization at death, then that gift will have an effect on what assets may be tapped to provide retirement income.

Medical Costs

Projecting medical costs in retirement is difficult. As a person ages, medical costs increase. Factors to evaluate include available health insurance, the cost of premiums, prescription drug coverage and overall state of health.

Long-term care needs - Expenses for long-term care as an individual ages should be considered as part of any sound retirement plan. A long stay in a nursing home can blow a large hole in an otherwise sound retirement plan. Long-term care insurance is a major expense that should be explored as part of the planning process. State and federal governments have tightened requirements for qualifying for Medicaid coverage of long-term expenses.

Social Security

Social Security is primarily the Old-Age, Survivors, and Disability Insurance (OASDI) federal program. The original Social Security Act (1935) and the current version of the Act, as amended, encompass several social welfare and social insurance programs. Social Security is funded through payroll taxes called Federal Insurance Contributions Act tax (FICA) and/or Self Employed Contributions Act Tax (SECA). With a few exceptions, all salaried income, up to a specifically determined amount by law (see tax rate table below) has an FICA and/or SECA tax collected on it. All income over said amount is not taxed, for 2021 the maximum amount of taxable earnings is $142,800.

Social Security Wage Base 2021	$142,800
Earnings Limit (under full retirement age)	$18,960/yr. ($1,520/mo.)
Earnings Limit (at full retirement age)	$50,520/yr. ($4,050/mo.)
Maximum Social Security benefit (FRA) in 2020	$3,148/mo.

- **Definition** - Social Security uses a strict definition of disability. The condition making an individual unable to work must be "severe" and the condition must prevent the individual from doing any type of work, not just the person's current occupation An individual may qualify to collect benefits under a private disability policy but be ineligible to collect Social Security disability benefits.
- **Eligibility** - There are two earnings tests to qualify for Social Security disability benefits: A "recent work" test based on age at

time of disability. A "duration of work" test to show an individual worked long enough under Social Security.

- **Benefits** - Payment of benefits begins are paid upon the sixth full month after the disability begins. The amount of benefit depends upon the worker's average lifetime earnings.
- **Death payment** - A spouse or minor children may be paid a one-time death benefit of $255 upon the death of a covered individual.
- **Family limitations**
  There is a limit on the amount of retirement, disability or survivor benefits payable to an entire family based on any one worker's record. This limit is known as the **maximum family benefit.**

Social Security Taxes (Paying into the System)
Workers and their employers are taxed on wages and other compensation up to an annual limit to pay for Social Security benefits. Self-employed individuals pay both the worker's and the employer's shares of the Social Security tax.

Social Security Taxes

Employee Pays	6.2%
Employer Pays	6.2%
Self Employed Pays	12.4%

Medicare taxes - In addition to Social Security taxes, workers also pay Medicare taxes on their compensation. There is no compensation limit for Medicare taxes.

Medicare Tax Rates

Employee Pays	1.45%
Employer Pays	1.45%
Self-Employed Pays	2.9%

Eligibility and Benefit

Assuming Normal Retirement Age of 65

	Retirement	Survivorship		Disability
	Fully Insured (2)	Fully Insured (2)	Currently Insured (3)	Disability Insured (4)
Participant-Age 65	100%	N/A	N/A	100%
Participant - Age 62	80%	N/A	N/A	100%
Dependent, Unmarried Child Under Age 18	50%	75%	75%	50%
Spouse with child under 16	50%	75%	75%	50%
Spouse-Age 65 (1)	50%	100%	0%	50%
Spouse-Age 62 (1)	37.50%	83%	0%	37.50%
Spouse-Age 60 (1)	N/A	71.50%	0%	N/A
Dependent Parent	0%	75/82.5 (5)	0%	0%

(1) Includes divorced spouse who has been married 10 years (unless they have remarried)
(2) Quarter of coverage is $1,470 in 2021
(3) Fully insured is 40 quarters of coverage
(4) Currently insured is at least six quarters of coverage in the last 13 quarters
(5) Disability insured is based on age as follows:
Before Age 24 – Must have 6 quarters of coverage in the last 12 quarters
Age 24 Through 30-Must be covered for half of the available quarters after age 21
Age 31 or Older – Must be fully insured and have 20 quarters of coverage in the last 40 quarters.
(6) Parent benefit is 82.5% for one parent, and 75% for each parent if two parents.

Calculating Benefits

1. Social Security benefits are typically computed using "average indexed monthly earnings." This average summarizes up to 35 years of a worker's indexed earnings. We apply a formula to this

average to compute the primary insurance amount (PIA). The PIA is the basis for the benefits that are paid to an individual. The formula used to compute the PIA reflects changes in general wage levels, as measured by the national average wage index.

2. Average Indexed Monthly Earnings (AIME)
When we compute an insured worker's benefit, we first adjust or "index" his or her earnings to reflect the change in general wage levels that occurred during the worker's years of employment. Such indexation ensures that a worker's future benefits reflect the general rise in the standard of living that occurred during his or her working lifetime. Up to 35 years of earnings are needed to compute average indexed monthly earnings. After we determine the *number* of years, we choose those years with the highest indexed earnings, sum such indexed earnings, and divide the total amount by the total number of months in those years. We then round the resulting average amount down to the next lower dollar amount. The result is the *AIME*.

3. The PIA is the sum of three separate percentages of portions of the AIME. While the percentages of this PIA formula are fixed by law, the dollar amounts in the formula change annually with changes in the national average wage index. The PIA is the sum of three separate percentages of portions of the AIME. While the percentages of this PIA formula are fixed by law, the dollar amounts in the formula change annually with changes in the national average wage index. These dollar amounts, called "bend points," govern the portions of the AIME. Monthly retirement benefits derived from the PIA may be higher or lower than the PIA. We pay reduced benefits to anyone who retires before his/her normal retirement age. A person cannot collect retirement benefits before age 62. In the case of a person retiring at exactly age 62 in 2020, the benefit will be 25 percent less than the person's PIA. Benefits can be higher than the PIA if one retires after the normal retirement age. The credit given for delayed retirement will gradually reach 8 percent per year for those born after 1942

4. Monthly retirement benefits derived from the PIA may be higher or lower than the PIA. We pay reduced benefits to one who retires before his/her normal retirement age. A person cannot collect retirement benefits before age 62.

Early Retirement

Workers may start receiving benefits as early as age 62, but their benefits are reduced permanently if they begin collecting them before full retirement age.

When taking retirement benefits early, the PIA is reduced five-ninths of 1% per month for each of the first 36 months that the worker takes before his FRA, plus five five-twelfths of 1% for each month in excess of 36 months.

Early Retirement Percentage	
Months Early	**Benefit Percentage**
6	96.67
12	93.33
18	90.00
24	86.67
30	83.33
36	80.00
42	77.5
48	75
54	72.5
60	70

Example:

Age	Benefit Received
Full retirement age 65	100%
Early retirement at 64	10% Reduction
Early retirement at 63	15% Reduction
Early retirement at 62	20% Reduction

Delaying Retirement

Social Security retirement benefits are increased by a certain percentage (depending on date of birth) if you delay your retirement beyond full retirement age. The benefit increase no longer applies when you reach age 70, even if you continue to delay taking benefits.

Increase for Delayed Retirement

Year of Birth	Yearly Rate of Increase	Monthly Rate of Increase
1933-1934	5.50%	11/24 of 1%
1935-1936	6.00%	1/2 of 1%
1937-1938	6.50%	13/24 of 1%
1939-1940	7.00%	7/12 of 1%
1941-1942	7.50%	5/8 of 1%
1943 or later	8.00%	2/3 of 1%

Taxation of Benefits

Recipients of Social Security retirement benefits pay taxes on their benefits if their non-Social Security income plus half of their Social Security benefits are above specified levels known as the base amount. This base amount varies by filing status. Generally, up to 50% of benefits are taxable. In the following situations, up to 85% of benefits may be taxable: Total of one half of benefits plus all other income exceeds $34,000 ($44,000 if married filing jointly). Benefits a recipient who is married, filing separately and lived with spouse at any time during the tax year.

No one pays federal income tax on more than 85 percent of his or her Social Security benefits based on Internal Revenue Service (IRS) rules. If you:

file a federal tax return as an "individual" and your *combined income** is

- between $25,000 and $34,000, you may have to pay income tax on up to 50 percent of your benefits.

- more than $34,000, up to 85 percent of your benefits may be taxable.

file a joint return, and you and your spouse have a *combined income** that is

- between $32,000 and $44,000, you may have to pay income tax on up to 50 percent of your benefits
- more than $44,000, up to 85 percent of your benefits may be taxable.

are married and file a separate tax return, you probably will pay taxes on your benefits.

> **Knowledge Nugget:**
> Your adjusted gross income
> + Nontaxable interest
> + ½ of your Social Security benefits
> = Your "**combined income**"

Types of Retirement Plans

Qualified Defined Benefit Plans

A defined benefit pension plan is a type of pension plan in which an employer/sponsor promises a specified monthly benefit on retirement that is predetermined by a formula based on the employee's earnings history, tenure of service and age, rather than depending directly on individual investment returns.

Defined Benefit Plan (Pension)

A defined benefit pension plan is a type of pension plan in which an employer/sponsor promises a specified monthly benefit on retirement that is predetermined by a formula based on the employee's earnings history, tenure of service and age, rather than depending directly on individual investment returns. A defined benefit plan has distinct characteristics. The plan objective is to provide a defined level of retirement income to each employee regardless of age at plan entry.

- The Employer promises to pay specified benefit at retirement
- The Employer bears investment risk
- Individual accounts are not established
- The Employer is allowed to deduct contributions up to the required funding amount
- Employees are allowed to defer income
- Employees (usually) does not contribute to the plan
- The maximum benefit allowable is 100% of compensation (based on the highest consecutive three-year average) to an indexed maximum annual benefit ($230,000 in 2021).
- A defined benefit plan may permit employees to elect to receive the benefit in a form other than monthly benefits, such as a lump sum payment

There are a few disadvantages of a defined benefit plan. Actuarial and Pension Benefit Guaranty Corporation (PBGC) of defined benefit plans result in higher installation and administration cost for defined contribution plans. They are also complex to design.

Cash Balance Plan (Pension)

A cash balance pension plan is a type of defined benefit plan that incorporates features similar to a defined contribution plan. The plan provides for annual employer contributions at a specified rate to hypothetical individual accounts that are maintained for each plan participant. The employer guarantees not only the contribution level but also a minimum rate of return on each participants account. The rate of return may be fixed or tied to a market rate, such as a Treasury rate.

- Employer bears only the investment risk up to a set rate of return
- Example: Guarantees 7% return on plan assets
- Benefits are limited by the DB rules

- $230,000 benefit in 2021 upon retirement at age 62 for any employee
- Cash balance plans must use three-year cliff vesting.

A cash balance plan pension plan is appropriate when the employee group is relatively young, when employees are concerned with security of retirement income, when the work force is large and the employees are primarily middle-income wage earners, and when the employer is able to spread administrative cost over a relatively large group of plan participants.

The rate of return allocated to participants in a Cash Balance Plan is guaranteed and is not dependent on the plan's investment performance. The rate of return allocated to participants changes each year and is usually equal to the yield on the 30-year Treasury bond, which in recent years has been around 5%. If the actual investment earnings exceed the amount allocated to participants (the guaranteed rate), the excess will be used to reduce future employer contributions in the following years. Excess returns are not credited to the participants' accounts.

Conversely if the plan's investment earnings are less than the amount necessary to meet the guaranteed rate, then future employer contributions will be increased to make up the difference. Shortfalls are typically amortized over five years.

Qualified Defined Contribution (Pension) Plans

Money Purchase Plan (Pension)

A money purchase pension is a qualified defined contribution retirement plan. The employers make annual mandatory contribution to each employee's account under a nondiscriminatory contribution formula. Contributions are further limited to the lesser of 100% of the employee's compensation of $58,000 (2021).

- Employer required to make contributions based upon contribution formula

- Plan is subject to minimum funding standards (whether or not the company has a profit)
- Employer minimum funding contributions are deductible
- Deduction limited to 25% of participating payroll

A money purchase plan is appropriate with an employer who wants to install a qualified retirement plan that is simple to administer and easy to explain to employees, and the employer does not mind mandatory funding. A money purchase plan is also appropriate when employees are willing to accept the investment risk in their plan accounts.

Target Benefit Plan (Pension)

- Combines DC and DB plan features
- Employee still bears investment risk
- Employer makes annual contributions
- Amounts are actuarially allocated based upon participant's age and compensation
- Plan allows older employees to accumulate wealth faster
- Deduction limited to 25% of participating payroll
- Annual additions limited to lesser of 100% of compensation or $58,000 per participant per year in 2021

Target benefit plans are appropriate when the client has a stable cash flow, and wants additional funds allocated to older employees.

Qualified Defined Contribution Plans

A **defined contribution (DC)** plan is a type of retirement plan in which the employer, employee or both make contributions on a regular basis. Individual accounts are set up for participants and benefits are based on the amounts credited to these accounts (through employer contributions and, if applicable, employee contributions) plus any investment earnings on the money in the account.

Profit Sharing (Defined Contribution Plans)

Profit Sharing Plans

A profit-sharing plan is a qualified defined contribution plan featuring a flexible employer contribution provision. The employer's contribution to the plan each year can be either a purely discretionary amount or based on some type of formula usually relating to the employer's annual profits. Contributions are generally allocated on the basis of nondiscriminatory formula and age-weighted formulas can be used to determine contributions. Profit-sharing plans may permit in-service distributions for a variety of reason such as medical expenses or a home purchase. For profit sharing plans to remain viable, contributions must be substantial and recurring.

- Employees bear all investment risk
- Employer minimum funding contributions are deductible
- Deduction limited to 25% of participating payroll
- Annual additions limited to lesser of 100% of compensation or $58,000 per participant per year in 2021

Stock Bonus Plan

A stock bonus plan is a type of profit-sharing plan. The major different between a stock bonus plan and a traditional profit-sharing plan is that stock bonus plan benefits are generally distributed in the form of employer stock and not cash. Annual additions limited to lesser of 100% of compensation or $58,000 per participant per year in 2021

- Employer contributions either made in company stock or used to purchase company stock
- Nondiscriminatory allocation of contributions
- Basis in stock treated as ordinary income and all appreciation taxed as capital gain when the employee sells the stock

A stock bonus plan is appropriate for a client who has treasury stock

Stock bonus plans may not be established by

- Partnerships

- Self-employed individuals
- ESOPs
- Employer contributions
- Contributions are deductible up to 25% of participating payroll 2020

The vesting schedule for a Defined Contribution Plan is as follows.

Employee contributions are 100% vested at all times.

Employer contributions to a defined contribution plan must use either the 3-year cliff vesting or 6 year graded vesting schedules.

Employee Stock Ownership Plan (ESOP)

An employee stock ownership plan (ESOP) is an IRC section 401(a) qualified defined contribution plan that is a stock bonus plan or a stock bonus/ money purchase plan. An ESOP must be designed to invest primarily in qualifying employer securities as defined by IRC section 4975(e)(8) and meet certain requirements of the Code and regulations. The IRS and Department of Labor share jurisdiction over some ESOP features.

401K

A 401(k) is a feature of a qualified profit-sharing plan that allows employees to contribute a portion of their wages to individual accounts.

- Elective salary deferrals are excluded from the employee's taxable income (except for designated Roth deferrals).
- Employers can contribute to employees' accounts.
- Distributions, including earnings, are includible in taxable income at retirement (except for qualified distributions of designated Roth accounts).

Roth 401K

- Designated Roth employee elective contributions are made with *after-tax dollars*

- No income limitation to participate.
- *Aggregate** employee elective contributions limited to $19,500 in 2021 plus an additional $6,500 for employees age 50 or over

Withdrawals of contributions and earnings are **not** taxed provided it's a **qualified distribution** – the account is held for at least 5 years and made:

1. On account of disability,
2. On or after death, or
3. On or after attainment of age 59½.
4. Distributions must begin no later than age 72, unless still working and not a 5% owner.

SIMPLE 401K

The SIMPLE 401(k), which has requirements similar to the SIMPLE IRA, can have a Roth 401(k) component. The employees must be totally vested in all of the contributions. Under a SIMPLE 401(k) plan, an employee can elect to defer some compensation. But unlike a regular 401(k) plan, you the employer must make either:

1. A matching contribution up to 3% of each employee's pay, or
2. A non-elective contribution of 2% of each eligible employee's pay

No other contributions can be made. The employees are totally vested in *any and all contributions.*

If you establish a SIMPLE 401(k) plan, you:

- Must have 100 or fewer employers.
- Cannot have any other retirement plans.
- Need to annually file a Form 5500.

Safe Harbor 401K Plan

The Safe Harbor rules are designed for 401(k) and 403(b) plans. These rules call for a company to make a specific contribution to each participant in the plan. If the rules are followed, a Safe Harbor 401(k) o

403(b) plan is allowed a free pass on the Actual Deferral Percentage (ADP) test, the Actual Contribution Percentage (ACP) test and the Top-Heavy minimum contributions.

A Non-Elective contribution to all eligible participants: a minimum of 3% of pay must include pay for the entire plan year regardless of the employee's entry date in the plan.

A matching contribution under one of the formulas listed below (*a match is allocated only to employees who defer their own pay to the plan*)

Basic Match: 4% of pay for participants who defer at least 5% of their pay. The Basic Match is structured as follows:

- 100% of the first 3% of pay that is contributed; and
- 50% of the next 2% of pay that is contributed

The Enhanced Match: 100% of the first 4% of pay that is contributed to the plan (*this is the minimum required under this option*)

- 100% of the first 6% of pay is the maximum allowed to still get a pass on the ACP test

Age-Based Profit-Sharing Plan

An age-based profit-sharing plan is a new type of tax qualified retirement plan which has two very special advantages. Age-based profit-sharing plans offer much larger contributions for older and highly paid owners and employees and permits the year-to-year discretionary contribution flexibility. Traditional profit-sharing plan contributions are determined based upon compensation without reference to the participant's age. Age-based profit-sharing plans is a cross-tested plan and use age and compensation in order to allocate contributions. Age-based profit-sharing plans permit older and highly paid owners to receive a greater contribution than traditional profit sharing plans.

New Comparability Profit Sharing Plan

A new comparability plan is a qualified profit-sharing plan that can have more substantial contributions for favored employees (usually higher-paid workers and key employees). With this type of plan, contributions are not allocated strictly as a percentage of compensation. Instead, by dividing up plan participants into two or more classes and having different contribution rates for each class, this type of plan allows businesses to maximize plan contributions for certain employees and minimize allocations to other employees. A new comparability plan satisfies nondiscrimination requirements by requiring minimum contributions and then having the plan pass a series of tests to show that the projected benefits for each class meet the coverage requirements. In general, a new comparability plan is a type of profit-sharing plan that is similar to an age-weighted plan in that both types of plans allow a business to maximize the plan contributions to the older, higher-paid owners and key employees while minimizing allocations to the accounts of younger employees.

New comparability plans, however, take this one step further than age-weighted plans by also putting employees into different groups or categories (rather than strictly using age) and each category may have a different contribution formula. As an employer with a new comparability plan, you may be able to provide yourself and other highly compensated employees a higher percentage of the plan contribution than you could under a traditional profit-sharing plan or even an age-weighted plan. You might also decide to receive the same dollar amount of a contribution as under a traditional profit-sharing plan but reduce the overall contribution amount for other employees.
The new comparability plan will only satisfy nondiscrimination rules if the plan design satisfies one of two minimum gateways:

- Each eligible non-HCE must receive an allocation of at least 5% of compensation
- If the plan provides an allocation rate of less than 5%, the minimum allocation rate for non-HCEs is one-third of the highest allocation rate under the plan.

Example: If the top allocation rate is 9%, the minimum allocation rate for non-HCEs would be 3% (9% divided by 3).

Thrift Savings Plan

The Thrift Savings Plan (TSP) is a retirement savings and investment plan for Federal employees and members of the uniformed services, including the Ready Reserve. It was established by Congress in the Federal Employees' Retirement System Act of 1986 and offers the same types of savings and tax benefits that many private corporations offer their employees under 401(k) plans.

The TSP is a defined contribution plan, meaning that the retirement income you receive from your TSP account will depend on how much you (and your agency, if you are eligible to receive agency contributions) put into your account during your working years and the earnings accumulated over that time. By participating in the TSP, Federal employees have the opportunity to save part of their income for retirement, receive matching agency contributions, and reduce their current taxes.

Keogh Plan

A Keogh plan is a tax-deferred pension plan available to self-employed individuals or unincorporated businesses for retirement purposes. A Keogh plan can be set up as either a defined-benefit or defined-contribution plan, although most plans are defined by contributions. Contributions are generally tax deductible up to a certain percentage of annual income with applicable absolute limits in U.S. dollar terms, which can be changed from year to year by the U.S. Internal Revenue Service (IRS).

Keogh plans can be set up as qualified defined-contribution plans, in which the contributions are made on a regular basis up to a limit. Profit-sharing plans are one of the two types of Keogh plans that allow a business to contribute up to 25% of compensation or $58,000 in 2020. A business does not have to generate profits to set aside money for this type of plan.

Qualified defined-benefit plans state the annual benefits to be received at retirement, and these benefits are typically based on salary and years of employment. Contributions towards defined-benefit Keogh plans are based on stated benefits and other factors, such as age and expected returns on plan assets. The IRS stated that in 2021, the maximum annual benefit is set at $230,000 or 100% of the employee's compensation, whichever is lower.

Other Tax-advantaged Retirement Plans

Traditional IRA

A traditional IRA is a way to save for retirement that gives you tax advantages.
Contributions you make to a traditional IRA may be fully or partially deductible, depending on your circumstances, and generally, amounts in your traditional IRA (including earnings and gains) are not taxed until distributed.

- Tax-deferred growth
- Contributions may be tax-deductible
- Maximum contribution for 2021: $6,000 ($7,000 if you are 50 or older) or 100% of employment compensation, whichever is less
- Under age 72 with employment compensation
- RMDs starting at 72
- No income limits to make contributions

Roth IRA

The Roth version of the individual retirement account (IRA) lets investors put away $6,000 in 2021; those over age 50 can put in an extra $1,000 in catch-up contributions. But that's no different from the traditional IRA. The significant differences between the Roth and the traditional IRA hinge on when you pay taxes and how much money ultimately goes to the government.

You cannot deduct contributions to a Roth IRA.

- There is an AGI phase-out for contribution.
- If you satisfy the requirements, qualified distributions are tax-free.

- You can make contributions to your Roth IRA after you reach age 72.
- You can leave amounts in your Roth IRA as long as you live.
- The account or annuity must be designated as a Roth IRA when it is set up.

Knowledge Nugget: Roth IRA contributions aren't deductible.

Simple IRA

A SIMPLE IRA plan (**S**avings **I**ncentive **M**atch **PL**an for **E**mployees) allows employees and employers to contribute to traditional IRAs set up for employees. It is ideally suited as a start-up retirement savings plan for small **(100 or less employees only)** employers not currently sponsoring a retirement plan. Generally, your plan should include any employee who received at least $5,000 in compensation from you during any two preceding calendar years, and is expected to receive at least $5,000 in compensation in the current calendar year.

An employee (including a self-employed individual) who:

- earned at least $5,000 in compensation during any 2 years before the current calendar year and
- expects to receive at least $5,000 during the current calendar year

An employer can exclude the following employees from a SIMPLE IRA plan:

- Employees covered by a union agreement and whose retirement benefits were bargained for in good faith by the employees' union and the employer
- Nonresident alien employees who do not have U.S. wages, salaries or other personal services compensation from the employer

Employee salary reduction contributions (elective deferrals)

- limited to $13,500 in 2021*

- For employees age 50 or over, a 3,000 "catch-up" contribution is also allowed in 2021)*

Employer contributions. The employer must annually choose one of the contribution methods below. The employer must tell employees during the election period which method will be used for the following year:

- **2% non-elective contribution** - 2% of each eligible employee's compensation regardless of whether or how much the employee deferred, or
- **3% matching contribution** - match of employee's elective deferrals on a dollar-for-dollar basis up to 3% of the employee's compensation.
- May reduce the 3% limit to a lower percentage, but in any event, not lower than 1%. May not lower the 3% limit for more than 2 calendar years out of the 5-year period ending with the calendar year the reduction is effective.

403(b) Plan

A 403(b) plan, also known as a tax-sheltered annuity (TSA) plan, is a retirement plan for employees of public schools, certain tax-exempt organizations, and certain ministers. 403(b) plan accounts can be any of the following types: (1) an annuity contract, which is provided through an insurance company; (2) a custodial account, which is invested in mutual funds; or (3) a retirement income account set up for church employees. Generally, retirement income accounts can invest in either annuities or mutual funds. Individual accounts in a 403(b) plan can be any of the following types.

We use the term "403(b) account" to refer to any one of these funding arrangements throughout this publication, unless otherwise specified.

SEP

Simplified Employee Pension (SEP) plans can provide a significant source of income at retirement by allowing employers to set aside mone in retirement accounts for themselves and their employees. Under a SEP, an employer contributes directly to traditional individual retirement accounts (SEP-IRAs) for all employees (including themselves). A SEP does not have the start-up and operating costs of a conventional retirement plan and allows for a contribution of up to 25 percent of each employee's pay or a maximum of $58,000 for 2021. A business of any size, even self-employed, can establish a SEP.

- Must be sole proprietor, a business owner, in a partnership, or earn self-employment income by providing a service
- Contributions must be made by the employer
- April 15 tax filing deadline for most self-employed individuals and small-business owners (including any extensions)
- Each employee must open an individual SEP IRA account.
- Minimum required distributions starting at age 72
- 10% early withdrawal penalty if under age 59½, subject to certain exceptions
- Investment options includes a wide range of mutual funds, stocks, bonds, ETFs, and FDIC-insured CDs

Eligible Employee – An eligible employee is an employee who:

- Is at least age 21, and
- Has performed service for you in at least 3 of the last 5 years.

All eligible employees must participate in the plan, including part-time employees, seasonal employees, and employees who die or terminate employment during the year.

Your SEP may also cover the following employees, but there is no requirement to cover them:

- Employees covered by a union contract;
- Nonresident alien employees who did not earn income from you;
- Employees who received less than $600 in compensation during the year (subject to cost-of-living adjustments).

Retirement Planning Regulatory Considerations

Employee Retirement Income Security Act of 1974 (ERISA)

The Employee Retirement Income Security Act of 1974 (ERISA) is a federal law that sets minimum standards for most voluntarily established pension and health plans in private industry to provide protection for individuals in these plans.

ERISA requires plans to provide participants with plan information including important information about plan features and funding; provides fiduciary responsibilities for those who manage and control plan assets; requires plans to establish a grievance and appeals process for participants to get benefits from their plans; and gives participants the right to sue for benefits and breaches of fiduciary duty.

Pension Benefit Guaranty Corporation (PBGC)

PBGC is a federal agency created by the Employee Retirement Income Security Act of 1974 (ERISA) to protect pension benefits in private-sector defined benefit plans - the kind that **typically** pay a set monthly amount at retirement. If your plan ends (this is called "plan termination") without sufficient money to pay all benefits, PBGC's insurance program will pay you the benefit provided by your pension plan up to the limits set by law. (Most people receive the full benefit they had earned before the plan terminated.) The financing comes from insurance premiums paid by companies whose plans the PBGC protects, from its investments, from the assets of pension plans that PBGCtake over as trustee, and from recoveries from the companies formerly responsible for the plans, but not from taxes. Your plan is insured even if your employer fails to pay the required premiums.

Economic Growth and Tax Relief Reconciliation Act (EGTRRA) of 2001

The Economic Growth and Tax Relief Reconciliation Act of 2001 (EGTRRA) made sweeping changes to wealth transfer taxation. The act gradually phased out the estate and generation-skipping transfer (GST) taxes and completely eliminated both in 2010, leaving only the gift tax (at a reduced rate) in that year.

Pension Protection Act of 2006

This legislation requires companies who have underfunded their pension plans to pay higher premiums to the Pension Benefit Guaranty Corporation (PBGC) and extends the requirement of providing extra funding to the pension systems of companies that terminate their pension plans. It also requires companies to analyze their pension plans' obligations more accurately, closes loopholes that previously allowed some companies to underfund their plans by skipping payments, and raises the cap on the amount employers are allowed to invest in their own plans. This will allow employers to deduct more money using the pension tax shield in times of high profits. It requires actuaries to use the equivalent of the projected accrued benefit cost method for determining annual normal cost.

Other Provisions:

- Provides statutory authority for employers to enroll workers in defined contribution plans automatically; formerly, the authority came from DOL rulemaking
- Expands disclosure that workers have about the performance of their pensions
- Removes the conflict-of-interest fiduciary liability from giving self-interested investment advice for retirement accounts
- Gives workers greater control over how their accounts are invested
- Allows automatic contributions to be returned to employees without tax penalties, if employee opts out within 90 days
- Established safe harbor investments, also known as Qualified Default Investment Alternatives, to protect employers from liability of losses suffered by automatically enrolled employees.

Chapter 10

Estate Planning

Characteristics and Consequences of Property Titling

In the law, title has a specific definition and means the legal evidence of a person's ownership rights in property. You can own two forms of property: 1) real property and 2) personal property. ***Real property*** is land and anything growing on, attached to, or erected on it. For example, your farmland, crops growing on the farmland, and any barns on the farmland would be considered real property. ***Personal property*** is a movable or intangible object subject to ownership and not classified as real property. For example, personal property would include farm equipment, tools, or company stock you might own.

Sole ownership: Sole ownership may be described as ownership by an individual or other entity capable of acquiring title.

Community property: In community property states, the division of property may be in the form of one spouse retaining title to certain marital assets, such as the house or a vacation home, and the other receiving a combination of some assets and a cash payment designed to make up any difference in value so that each person leaves the marriage with an equal amount in marital property. Note that debts are considered marital property, and are split evenly in a community property state. The nine community property states are below:

- Arizona
- California
- Idaho
- Louisiana
- Nevada
- New Mexico
- Texas
- Washington
- Wisconsin

Not all property the couple owns is considered marital property. Anything that is not considered marital property is not divided equally in community property states. Marital property excludes:

- Anything acquired before the marriage or after the date of separation
- Cash received by one of the spouses as a gift or inheritance as long as it is deposited in a separate bank account in one spouse's name only
- Property received by one of the spouses as a gift or inheritance as long as the property is in one spouse's name only and not mixed with other marital assets

Joint Tenancy with Right of Survivorship (JTWROS) is an interest in property held by two or more related or unrelated persons called joint tenants. Each person holds an undivided, equal interest in the whole property. Each joint tenant shares equally in the income and expenses of the property in proportion to his interest. A rights of survivorship is normally implied with this form of ownership, and at the death of the first joint tenant, the decedent's interest transfers to the other joint tenants outside of the probate process according to state titling law.

Tenancy in Common (TIC) is an interest in property held by two or more related or unrelated persons. Each owner is referred to as a tenant in common tenancy in common is the most common type of joint ownership between non-spouses. Each person holds an undivided, but not necessarily equal, interest in the entire property. Each co-owner does not own a designated portion of the property, instead he owns an interest in the entire property.

Tenancy by the entirety (TE) tenancy by the entirety is very similar to joint tenancy between a husband and wife. To understand this form or ownership it is important to remember the following four key components:

- Tenancy by the entirety applies to joint ownership only between married couples.

- Neither tenant is able to sever their interest without the consent of the other tenant (spouse)
- Property ownership interest is automatically transferred to the surviving spouse upon death
- It may involve the ownership interest of real or personal property.

Strategies to Transfer Property

Probate

Probate refers to the process whereby certain of the decedent's debts may be settled and legal title to the decedent's property held in the decedent's name alone and not otherwise distributed by law is transferred to heirs and beneficiaries. If a decedent had a will, and the decedent had property subject to probate, the **probate process** begins when the executor, who is nominated by the decedent in the **last will**, presents the will for probate in a courthouse in the county where the decedent lived, or owned property. If there is no will, someone must ask the court to appoint him or her as administrator of the decedent's estate. Often, this is the spouse or an adult child of the decedent. Once appointed by the court, the executor or administrator becomes the legal representative of the estate.

The Four Basic Steps to Probate

1. File a petition and give notice to heirs and beneficiaries.

As described above, the probate process begins with the filing of the petition with the **probate court** to either (1) admit the will to probate and appoint the executor or (2) if there is no will, appoint an administrator of the estate. Generally, notice of the court hearing regarding the petition must be provided to all of the decedent's heirs and beneficiaries. If an heir or beneficiary objects to the petition, they have the opportunity to do so in court. Also, generally, notice of the hearing is published in a local newspaper.

This is to attempt to notify others, such as unknown creditors of the decedent, of the beginning of the proceeding.

2. Following appointment by the court, the personal representative must give notice to all known creditors of the estate and take an inventory of the estate property.

The personal representative then gives written notice to all creditors of the estate based upon state law; any creditor who wishes to make a claim on assets of the estate must do so within a limited period of time (which also varies by state).

An inventory of all of decedent's probate property, including real property, stocks, bonds, business interests, among other assets, is taken. In some states, a court appointed appraiser values the assets. When necessary, an independent appraiser is hired by the estate to appraise non-cash assets.

3. All estate and funeral expenses, debts and taxes must be paid from the estate.

The personal representative must determine which creditor's claims are legitimate and pay those and other final bills from the estate. In some instances, the personal representative is permitted to sell estate assets to satisfy the decedent's obligations.

4. Legal title in property is transferred according to the will or under the laws of intestacy (if the decedent did not have a will).

Following the waiting period to allow creditors to file claims against the estate, and all approved claims and bills are paid, generally, the personal representative petitions the court for the authority to transfer the remaining assets to beneficiaries as directed in the decedent's last will and testament or, if there is no will, according to state intestate succession laws. If the will calls for the creation of a trust for the benefit of a minor, spouse or incapacitated family member, money is then transferred to the trustee. Unless the beneficiaries of the estate waive the requirement as allowed under some state laws, the petition may include an accounting of how the assets were managed during the probate process. Once the petition is granted, the personal representative may draw up new deeds for property, transfer stock, liquidate assets and transfer property to the appropriate recipients.

In short, a properly drafted will, updated regularly to account for life changes, organized records of debts, personal property and other assets simplifies the probate process. The easier it is for your personal representative to trace your steps after you're gone, the easier the process.

Transfer at Death

Estate planning involves transfer of ownership at life and death. This section will focus on the transfer at death. There are four primary ways to transfer property ownership at death.

1) Transfers through the probate process (provisions in your will)
2) Transfers by operation of law
   - **Joint Tenants with Right of Survivorship (JTWROS)** Joint tenancy with rights of survivorship is commonly used between married couples. In this co-ownership, each party owns the property equally and undivided. If one party wishes to transfer his share to someone else during his lifetime, the other owner must consent and sign the resulting deed. The rights of survivorship imply that upon the death of one owner, his share is transferred automatically to the surviving owner. The survivorship rights take precedence over the deceased's will or inheritance rules.
   - **Joint Tenants in Common (TIC)** In a tenants in common ownership situation, two or more owners can own equal or unequal shares of the same property. For example, two owners can hold equal shares, or multiple owners can own different percentages that equal 100. The shares in ownership are separate from one another. So one owner can transfer his share to someone else at any point in time without the consent of the other owners. If an owner dies, his share in the property is passed along to the person named in his will or to his surviving heirs if no will exists.

- **Intestate Succession** If you die without making a will, a court will distribute your property according to the laws of your state. This process is called "intestate succession" or "intestacy." Who gets what depends on who your closest relatives are. The most likely recipients are your spouse, your children, your parents, or your siblings.

4) Transfers through trusts
5) Transfers by contract
    - Retirement plans
    - Annuities
    - Life insurance policies

Estate Planning Documents

Wills

Wills are one of the most basic instruments used to transfer property. In most states, the only requirements necessary to execute a valid will are:

1. The will must be in writing and
2. The will must be signed at its logical end by the testator.

Statutory wills are drawn by an attorney and comply with the statutes for wills of the domiciliary state. Statutory wills are generally witnessed and attested. Statutory wills must be typed or be in writing, be signed by the testator (A **testator** is a person who has written and executed a last will and testament that is in effect at the time of his/her death.) and be signed by the witnesses.

Holographic wills are handwritten by the testator and include the material provisions of a will. The holographic will must be dated and signed by the testator, but most stated do not require a witness. Holographic wills are valid in most states.

Nuncupative wills are oral, dying declarations made before a sufficient number of witnesses. In some states, nuncupative wills may only be effective to pass personal property, not real property, and the dollar amount transferred by this method may be limited. The use of a nuncupative wills is restrictive and is not valid in most states. In states when such wills are permitted, the witnesses must generally submit an affidavit declaring the testator's final wishes.

Codicil: When it's time to update your Will, you don't have to start from scratch. You can create a Codicil to a Will to revise your Will when you get married, divorced or have a child, among other reasons. Use our Codicil to Will to ensure the changes to your Will are legal and enforceable.

Letter of Instruction
A letter of instruction is an informal document that gives your survivors information concerning important financial and personal matters that must be attended to after your death. There is no requirement for an attorney to prepare a letter of instruction. The letter of instruction does not carry the weight of a will and is no way a substitute for a will, a letter of instruction clarifies any special request to be carried out upon death.

Living Will
Living wills and other advance directives are written, legal instructions regarding your preferences for medical care if you are unable to make decisions for yourself. Advance directives guide choices for doctors and caregivers if you're terminally ill, seriously injured, in a coma, in the late stages of dementia or near the end of life.

Powers of Attorney
Power of Attorney form (also known as a POA) allows you to give legal permission to someone else to act on your behalf. A durable power of attorney will remain in effect when the writer of the power of attorney becomes incapacitated. You can give someone the ability to write checks, sign official documents or handle other legal matters on your behalf. Whether you're going to be unavailable, or you want to prepare for unexpected illness or incapacity, create a Power of Attorney to make sure the right person makes decisions for you.

- You want to grant authority to someone to act on your behalf in your absence.

- You want to grant authority to someone to act on your behalf in the event you become incapacitated.
- You want to grant authority to someone to act on your behalf in specific situation.

Powers Of Appointment
The power of appointment (POA) over property is the right of the holder of the power to specify who will be the recipient of the enjoyment and use of the property subject to the power.

There are three primary terms associated with the POA:
1) Appointee – Property recipient
2) Donor – Grantor of power over property
3) Donee – The holder of the power

General and Special (Limited) Powers
The "powers" are classified as either "General" or "Special" powers. If the holder can exercise their power without any restrictions or conditions attached, then the power is a general power. Under a special or "limited" power, the holder can only exercise their power under certain conditions, limited periods of time or for specific beneficiaries.

Gross Estate Inclusion:
1) General Powers - YES
2) Special Powers – NO

5-and-5 Power
The 5-and-5 Power is a general power of appointment that would not be included in the gross estate of the decedent if their power is limited to a "noncumulative right" to withdrawal the GREATER of the following:

1) $5,000, OR
2) 5%of the aggregate value of the property annually

This power is a valuable technique used by financial and estate planners to provide some financial benefit and flexibility to a beneficiary with little or no tax consequences.

Crummey Powers
A Crummey Power is commonly found in irrevocable trust documents, and used to allow the grantor to make annual gifts to the trust that will qualify under the federal gift tax exclusion ($15,000 per beneficiary/per year in 2020).

Qualifications under a "Crummey Power" for a non-taxable gift:
1) The gift must be given to the trust outright (no strings attached), and
2) The trustee must give reasonable notice to the beneficiaries that the gift was made and available for withdrawal

The right of withdrawal is limited to the LESSER of the amount of the annual exclusion OR the value of the gift transferred.

Distributions for an Ascertainable Standard
A special (limited) power of appointment will be assumed if the decedent has power over the trust to invade the principal to maintain an "ascertainable standard" or health, education, maintenance and support (“**HEMS**”) **standard**, as it is expressly referenced in Internal Revenue Code Section 2041(b)(1)(A). HEMS. This HEMS standard is commonly referred to as an “ascertainable standard” as it allows a trustee with parameters in which to make decisions regarding what distributions are appropriate for a particular trust beneficiary. In using this standard, a grantor can be assured that there will be a balance between the prevention of distributions for extravagant purposes and provision for the beneficiary’s needs.

"Ascertainable Standard" is: HEMS

- Health
- Education
- Maintenance
- Support

No general power is implied if the decedent only has the power to withdrawal corpus to maintain their well-being.

Health. The standard of "health" is generally thought to include the following: a. Emergency medical treatment;
b. Psychiatric treatment;
c. Psychological treatment;
d. Routine health care examinations;
e. Dental;
f. Eye care;
g. Cosmetic Surgery;
h. Lasik surgery;
i. Health, Dental, or Vision Insurance;
j. Unconventional medical treatment;
k. Home health care;
l. Gym memberships;
m. Spa memberships;
n. Golf club memberships; and
o. Extended vacations to relieve tension and stress.

2. **Education**. The standard of "education" is thought to include the following: a. Grammar, secondary and high school tuition;
b. Graduate school;
c. Post-graduate school;
d. Medical school, law school, or other professional school;
e. Support of the beneficiary while in school;
f. Support of beneficiary while not in school (between semesters);
g. Studies for the student that makes a career out of learning;
h. Technical school training;
i. Career training;
j. College in Europe as part of a study abroad program4; and
k. Related expenses such as supporting the beneficiary not only during the semester, but, also between semesters

3. **Support and Maintenance**. The terms "support" and "maintenance" are considered synonymous. When applied, these terms do not limit a trustee to providing merely the bare necessities in life but allow for significant discretion. To provide additional clarity, these terms are often used in conjunction with additional language, such as: "support in reasonable comfort," "maintenance in health and reasonable comfort,"

or "support in the beneficiary's accustomed manner of living." In addition, the Restatement of Trusts takes several notable positions with regard to what can fairly be interpreted to be permissible distributions pursuant to a "support and maintenance" standard. The list provided within the Restatement is specifically broken down into three categories: (1) what is generally deemed to be included, (2) what might be included, and (3) what expressly is not included.

a. Generally included:
   1. Regular mortgage payments;
   2. Property taxes;
   3. Suitable health insurance or care;
   4. Existing programs of life and property insurance;
   5. Continuation of accustomed patterns of vacation;
   6. Continuation of family gifting; and
   7. Continuation of charitable gifting.

b. Might be included:
   1. Reasonable additional comforts or luxuries; and
   2. Special vacations of a type the beneficiary had never taken before.

c. Not included:
   1. Payments unrelated to support which merely contribute to the beneficiary's contentment or happiness;
   2. Distributions to enlarge the beneficiary's personal estate

Lapse of Power

When a holder of a power of appointment loses control to determine which beneficiaries will benefit from the trust property, then a release of power of appointment has occurred. If a general power of appointment was not exercised within a specified period of time, it is considered to have lapsed.

Prenuptial Agreement

Premarital agreements (also called prenuptial agreements or "prenups") are a common legal step taken before marriage. A prenup establishes the property and financial rights of each spouse in the event of a divorce. So, while no one is thinking about a divorce when they get married, about one half of all marriages in America end up in divorce proceedings. So, it's often prudent to at least consider a prenuptial agreement. Prenups are often used to protect the assets of wealthy spouses but also can protect family businesses and serve other important functions. Create a Prenuptial Agreement to set a foundation for clear communication, protect your assets, avoid your spouse's debts and prevent conflicts should something happen.

Use a Prenuptial Agreement if:

- You are contemplating marriage and wish to explain rights and obligations of each person regarding property.
- You own significant amounts of property.
- You have previously been married.
- You have children from a prior marriage.

Postnuptial Agreement

A postnuptial agreement is a legal contract you enter into after marriage. The purpose of the agreement is to settle financial and marital issues that are present within the marriage. A postnuptial agreement can cover current and future debts. It can cover who owns which assets. It can also address mundane issues like the household budget and day-to-day concerns, such as how much time one spouse can devote to hobbies or hanging out with friends. A postnuptial agreement can exclude business debt from a future divorce. However, it cannot include a waiver of a spouse's obligation to pay child support.

Gift and Estate Tax

Gift Tax

The gift tax is a tax on the transfer of property by one individual to another while receiving nothing, or less than full value, in return. The tax applies whether the donor intends the transfer to be a gift or not. The gift tax applies to the transfer by gift of any property. You make a gift if you give property (including money), or the use of or income from property, without expecting to receive something of at least equal value in return. If you sell something at less than its full value or if you make an interest-free or reduced-interest loan, you may be making a gift.

Sources for Estate Liquidity

Estate Liquidity Needs

When a person dies, certain taxes and other debts must be paid within a short period of time. The taxes and costs lower the amount transferred to heirs and may include:

- Funeral expenses
- Expenses due to illness
- Debts of the decedent
- Probate and attorney costs
- Federal and state estate taxes

Estate Liquidity Sources

There may be shortfalls in estate liquidity needs due to insufficient cash assets or inadequate planning. To satisfy these liquidity needs the heirs of the decedent may have to sell the decedent assets, use of life insurance proceeds and loans.

Sale of Assets
Heirs may be able to sell off the decedent's assets, for example, a home or business. This may be a last resort as it usually results in losses because you are forced to sell. However, because the property was sold after death, the property will receive a step-up in cost basis, resulting in minimizing a gain.

Life Insurance
Life insurance may be used to provide the estate with sufficient cash to satisfy the claims of creditors and to pay the taxes and other costs resulting from death. For individuals whose estates will be subject to the federal estate tax, life insurance can also be arranged so that it is not included in the gross estate.
Advantages of life insurance include:

- Proceeds are available immediately when needed.
- Proceeds are received free of federal income tax.

- The policy can be arranged to avoid probate and federal estate tax.
- Borrowing the cash at interest is also avoided, including paying the federal estate tax in installments (see below).
- Policy death proceeds will nearly always equal more than premiums that were paid, allowing death costs to be funded for cents on the dollar.

  This is generally the most effective method to provide liquidity for an estate.

Loan - Installment Note

Heirs can also borrow funds to pay the debts owed. Also, if the estate assets are pledged or bonded as security, the heirs may not be able to enjoy them.

Types, Features, and Taxation of Trusts

Reason for Creating a Trust

- To avoid probate
- To reduce transfer or income taxes
- Asset management for an individual who is the grantor and the beneficiary in the case he becomes incapacitated
- To make charitable contributions while remaining some interest

Five Common Elements of all Trusts:

- Creator (Grantor, Settlor or Trustor)
- Trustee
- Beneficiaries
- Trust Property
- Terms of the Trust

Trust Characteristics

Trust funds fall within one of two categories in terms of how they're structured: simple and complex. The difference between the two has to do with when and how asset distributions occur. With a simple trust, beneficiaries can only receive accumulated interest from a fund account until a stated time period has passed. Once the time period passes, beneficiaries have access to both the principal and interest monies in an account. With a complex trust, beneficiaries can receive both principal and interest monies for as long as the trust exists, though a complex trust typically includes conditions for distribution time periods and amounts.

Revocable and Irrevocable

The Revocable Trust is a trust created by a grantor by transferring property to the trust under the supervision of a trustee(s). Some common reasons for creating a revocable trust include the following:

Revocable Trusts:

- Probate avoidance
- Monitor the trustee
- Gifting property in trust
- Grantor lacks time to manage
- Avoid out-of-state disputes
- Preserve a family business

The Irrevocable Trust is a trust created by a grantor whereas property is transferred to the trust permanently. The grantor will lose control and possession of the property. These trusts are frequently used to remove assets from an estate to reduce estate tax exposure.

Irrevocable Trusts:

- Probate avoidance
- Avoids the claims of grantor's creditors
- Shelter and protect assets
- Provide property for beneficiaries
- Gifting opportunities
- Estate tax reduction

Inter Vivos and Testamentary

Inter vivos is a Latin term meaning "between the living," so an inter vivos trust is a living trust that is created for use before the death of the grantor. It can be both revocable and irrevocable.

The testamentary trust is a trust created under the terms of a will, thus making them subject to probate. These trusts are considered revocable until the death of the testator; at the time of death it becomes irrevocable. Characteristics of a testamentary trust would include the following:

Testamentary Trusts:

- Grantor wants to maintain control of property
- No probate avoidance (public information)
- Irrevocable at death
- No estate or income tax savings during the life of the testator
- Distribution of property at death to multiple beneficiaries

Types and Basic Provisions of Trust

Totten Trust

The Totten Trust refers to certain types of accounts established at financial institutions that can be set up to pay to a certain beneficiary at the death of the account owner. These "payable on death" (POD) accounts are fully controlled by the owner during their lifetime, and consist of individual accounts located at banks and most brokerage firms. Individuals setting up these accounts as POD or TOD (transfer on death) enable the heirs of the account to avoid probate of the assets.

Spendthrift Trust

A Spendthrift Trust is a trust setup with "spendthrift provisions or clauses" that protect the trust assets and the beneficiary assets from creditors of the beneficiary. The trust is normally created to allow the trustee to control the distribution of the trust's assets to the beneficiary(s) in order to manage the spending habits of the beneficiary(s). The creator of the trust might also be afraid that the beneficiary would "blow through" the assets of the trust if a controlled budget and independent trustee was not in place to maintain stability.

Bypass Trust

The Bypass Trust, also known as the "B-Trust" or "Credit Shelter Trust," uses trust assets to provide the surviving spouse with income for the rest of his or her life, as well as principal from the trust for his or her healthcare expenses, education expenses and costs for his or her support and maintenance. This trust was primarily used to take advantage of the deceased's estate tax exemption amount whereas the assets placed in the trust would not be treated as being owned by the surviving spouse for tax purposes, and would therefore not be included in his or her estate for purposes of federal estate tax liability. Upon the surviving spouse's death, the assets could be passed to the trust's beneficiaries without estate tax.

Marital Trust

The Marital Trust, also known as the "A-Trust" or "Power of Appointment Trust," is a trust utilized by the grantor as an unlimited marital deduction trust to transfer assets to their spouse in the name of trust. The spouse is given the right to income for life and a general power of attorney over the trust's assets. If the spouse does not use all of the trust's assets over their lifetime, then the remaining assets will be includable as part of their taxable estate.

Qualified Terminable Interest Property (QTIP) Trust

The QTIP Trust is a marital trust set up by a grantor to transfer unlimited amounts of assets under the unlimited marital deduction to this trust for the benefit of the spouse. The spouse receives income for life from the trust, but is usually not given power of appointment. Generally, this trust is used by the grantor to take care of the surviving spouse for life (income from the trust), but in turn leave the trust's assets to children or other family members (corpus or principal). Assets are included in the estate of the surviving spouse at death; however, the trust can be used to pay the pro-rata share of estate tax due.

Pour-Over Trust

The Pour-Over Trust is a simple term meaning that property is transferred or "poured over" from an estate or another trust into a preexisting trust. If a pour-over will is established, it can be used to catch forgotten assets and direct them to be placed in the pour-over trust. To have legal effect, the trust must be in place prior to the creation of the will. Assets from other sources such as IRAs and insurance proceeds can also "pour-over" into this type of trust at the death of the creator.

Section 2503(b) Trust

The Section 2503(b) Trust is also known as the "Mandatory Income Trust" for minors. This irrevocable trust is established by the grantor to provide an annual income source for the care and welfare of a minor child. The income is taxable to the trust beneficiary (child) and the child does not have access to the trust's assets until adulthood. The donor may meet the requirements of annual gift tax exclusion.

Section 2503(c) Trust

The Section 2503(c) Trust is another irrevocable trust for minors. Both the income and principal distribution is discretionary until the minor becomes an adult. Income not paid out to the child is taxed at trust tax rates. Upon reaching the age of majority (age 21), the trust becomes the property of the now adult child. If the beneficiary elects to leave the property in the trust, they must still pay income taxes on the trust earnings even though it is not distributed to them.

Sprinkling Provision

Under a "sprinkling provision," the trustee can be authorized to distribute income of the trust among children and other beneficiaries based on their need or simply in the trustee's discretion. This flexibility allows the trustee to be tax sensitive to the beneficiaries needs, giving the trustee the power to distribute the income to the children beneficiaries or those in lower tax brackets.

Rabbi Trust

A rabbi trust is a trust established by an employer to provide a source of funds which may be used to satisfy the employer's obligation to executives under a nonqualified benefit plan. The trust is referred to as a rabbi trust because the first IRS letter ruling with respect to this type of trust involved a rabbi whose congregation had made contributions to such a trust for his benefit. The ruling stated that the rabbi would not be taxed on the funds in the trust until the funds were distributed to the rabbi (or his beneficiary) upon his death, disability, retirement, or termination of employment. Typically, the rabbi trust is set up as an *irrevocable trust* - the employer must give up all rights to the assets and may not terminate the trust. The trust is also usually considered a grantor trust, with income being taxed to the grantor or employer.

The main purpose of establishing a rabbi trust is to offer some level of security to the employee with respect to their nonqualified benefits. This is especially true for a Nonqualified Deferral Plan (NQDP), where the employee defers compensation with only a contractual promise of the employer to pay the benefits. Employee deferrals will be placed in the trust as deferrals are made. In the event a "locked" Rabbi Trust is established, once funds are placed in the trust, they may not revert to the employer until all benefit obligations are fully discharged. Trust assets must be used to pay benefits under the plan. An "unlocked" Rabbi Trust allows the corporation to access asset values as it sees fit.

Secular Trust

A secular trust is an irrevocable trust, usually established by the employer, that holds assets to be used for the exclusive purpose of providing funds for the payment of nonqualified benefits. The establishment of the secular trust provides additional security to participants over and above the rabbi trust, in that the assets in a secular trust are not subject to the claims of creditors. However, establishing a secular trust fundamentally changes the benefit structure as immediate taxation results. Typically, the after-tax value of a benefit is funded within a secular trust and the participating executive is generally provided additional bonus monies to satisfy the income tax consequences of the security established.

Thus, the security given is protection against:

- Change of heart: The employer cannot access assets in the trust, once committed.
- Change of control: An unfriendly takeover will not affect the assets in the trust.
- Creditors and bankruptcy: Assets are beyond the reach of creditors.

Taxation of Trust Income:

1) ***If passed to a beneficiary*** – Income is taxed to the beneficiary at their ordinary income tax rates.
2) ***If remaining in a trust*** – Income is taxed to the trust at trust income tax rates, which could be much higher than individual tax rates.
Trusts generally retain capital gains and losses since they are changes to the principal (corpus) of the trust. Therefore, they are not considered income for distribution purposes. The trust will report capital gains on its own tax return and pay the tax.

Rule against Perpetuities
Certain limitations were created to prevent property from being held in a trust indefinitely. The rule prevents the transferor of property from controlling the disposition of the property for unreasonably long periods of time while in the trust, commonly known as "ruling from the dead."

The rule states that: Interest in the property must vest no later than 21 years and 9 months once the trust becomes irrevocable.

Uniform Statutory Rule Against Perpetuities:
Several individual states have adopted the "uniform statutory rule against perpetuities" which extends the original rule of perpetuities out to 90 years.

Estate and Gift Taxation
The estate-gift tax exemption amount is $11,580,000 per person in 2020(or $23,160,000 per couple in 2020) with a top estate tax rate of 40% should an estate exceed those amounts.
Assets retained in revocable trusts are included as part of the gross estate for estate tax purposes- because the grantor retained control of the assets, they are still considered as assets of their estate. Irrevocable trusts can pass free of estate taxation if the grantor (creator) has given up all incidences of ownership.

Grantor Trust

Grantor Retained Annuity Trusts

A grantor retained annuity trust (GRAT) is an irrevocable trust for which the grantor retains the right to receive a fixed annual dollar amount or percentage of the initial assets deposited at least annually from the trust. The grantor usually transfers appreciating or income producing property to the trust in exchange for this "fixed annuity" type payout feature for a set number of years.

Characteristics of a GRAT:

- After the initial transfer of the property (gift) into the trust, no other additions are permitted.
- An excellent way to remove property from an estate utilizing the gift tax exclusion amounts.
- Provides a steady reliable income steam for the grantor for a set number of years.
- When the term of the GRAT ends, the remaining assets are transferred tax-free to the named beneficiaries.
- If the grantor does not out live the term of the trust, all of the property is brought back into the grantor's estate.

Grantor Retained UniTrusts

A grantor retained unitrust (GRUT) is another irrevocable trust where the grantor retains the right to receive funds annually from the trust based on a fixed percentage that is recalculated annually based on the new value of the trust. The grantor transfers property into the trust in exchange for a "variable annuity" type payout feature where the annual income stream will vary from year-to-year, depending on the value of the trust.

Characteristics of a GRUT:

- The grantor can make the initial gift and additional gifts to the trust.

- An excellent way to remove property from an estate utilizing the gift tax exclusion amounts.
- Provides a variable income stream to the grantor for a set number of years or for life.
- When the term of the GRUT ends, the remaining assets are transferred tax-free to the named beneficiaries.
- If the grantor does not out live the term of the trust, all of the property is brought back into the grantor's estate.

Qualified Personal Residence Trusts

A qualified personal residence trust (QPRT or House-GRITs) is used by a grantor to transfer their personal residence to a trust with the right to retain the use of the home for a specified number of years. At the termination of the trust, one or more remainder beneficiaries receive the personal residence.

Valuation of Qualified Interests

GRATs and GRUTs - Discounting may be used

The irrevocable transfer of the remaining interest in the GRAT or GRUT is considered a current gift for gift tax purposes. The gift does not qualify for the annual exclusion, but it is discounted from the fair market value of the corpus by subtracting the value of the grantor's retained interest.

Taxable Gift:

The retained interest value is determined based on the amount of the annual payment, payment term and the monthly percentage rate obtained from Section 7520 rules. The discounted gift can then be sheltered by the grantor's applicable credit amount.

Chapter 11

Major Life Purchases: Home and Car

Buying Versus Renting a Home

Buying a house instead of renting a place to live needs to make sense financially. Buying a house involves raising a down payment and paying a monthly mortgage for several years (usually 15 to 30 years). It also includes paying homeowner's insurance and taxes (and could involve Private Mortgage Insurance if your down payment is less than 20% of the loan). The **down payment is** the lump sum you'll pay upfront that funds equity in the property and proves to lenders that you've got skin in this homeowner game.

You can use many amortization calculators or online resources to see how many years it will take before the cost of buying equals the cost of renting. It's called the breakeven horizon, and it varies by area of the country. If you plan to stay in your home past your breakeven horizon, then buying makes financial sense. If you think you'll move earlier, then renting may be the way to go.

Down payments vary because there are so many financing options available. In the days that led up to the housing collapse in 2008, some lenders dismissed the down payment altogether – and we see how well that ended. Historically, 20 percent was preferred because it allowed borrowers to avoid paying Private Mortgage Insurance (PMI). PMI is typically required by lenders so that if the borrower defaults on the loan, the lender is made whole. If you have good credit, your lender may assess PMI premiums until your loan-to-value (LTV) ratio – the ratio of your current mortgage balance to your home's total value – reaches 78%. However, lenders generally honor borrowers' PMI cancellation requests once LTV reaches 80%. If you pose a higher credit risk, your lender may require you to carry PMI until your LTV is lower. If you are receiving assistance with your down payment from friends or family, take a gift rather than a loan, not only for obvious reasons, but because lenders will add that debt to other monthly obligations and potential mortgage payments to determine your debt-to-income ratio, which you generally want to keep below 43 percent to qualify for a home loan.

The monthly **mortgage** payment in most cases, includes the loan principal and interest (both amortized over the life of the loan) plus homeowner's insurance and property taxes (pro-rated) and potentially PMI (if the down payment is below 20%).

True Costs of Home Ownership

Up Front Cost of Home Ownership and Recurring Costs

When you initially begin making a deal for a new home to show the seller you're serious about buying the property, it's customary to accompany your purchase offer with an **"earnest money"** check. Earnest money generally ranges from 1% to 3% of the home's purchase price, depending on local market conditions and the seller's preference. After accepting the offer, the seller deposits the earnest money funds into an escrow account, and the amount is credited against your closing costs.

To ensure that the offer price does not exceed the actual value of the home, lenders require a home **appraisal** prior to approving the loan. Appraisal costs, typically $300 to $500, are paid during or before the appraisal. Licensed home inspectors are trained to find potential problems and defects that might not be apparent to an inexperienced buyer doing a casual walk-through. For this reason, buyers are strongly encouraged to get one, even though private lenders rarely make loan approval conditional on a completed home inspection. The cost is similar to the appraisal and is usually paid at the inspection.

Appraisal, inspection, taxes, and insurance are just a few of the many line items bundled into your closing. Other closing costs include loan origination charges, credit report fee, flood certification fee, lender's and owner's title insurance, recording taxes, state and local transfer taxes, first month's mortgage interest, and closing fee. As a rule of thumb, you can expect your total closing costs to range from 2% to 4% of the purchase price, with the ratio falling as the purchase price increases.

Homeowner's, have full responsibility for paying all utilities and local services (water, gas, electric, garbage and recycling, cable and Internet, etc.) on their property:. These costs vary widely by location and usage. In reality, the burden of all home maintenance and upkeep costs, such as replacing worn-out fixtures and appliances, exterior painting and finishing, interior cleaning, and mechanical maintenance (such as HVAC cleaning and inspection) fall on your shoulders. As a general rule of thumb, you can expect to pay 1% of your home's value per year on maintenance and wear-related replacements and repairs.

Special Costs of Homeownership

In addition to the known costs, homeownership also comes with somewhat less-predictable costs that occur only once or at irregular intervals. Such things as the cost of hiring movers, buying furniture and fixtures for the home as well as replacing carpet or remediating mold if you somehow sustain water damage from exterior flooding (if not properly insured).

Types of Home Loans

Fixed Rate Mortgages - A mortgage in which the interest rate remains the same throughout the entire life of the loan is a fixed rate mortgage. These loans are the most popular ones, representing over 75% of all home loans. They usually come in terms of 30, 15, or 10 years, with the 30-year option being the most popular. While the 30-year option is the most popular, a 15-year builds equity much faster. The biggest advantage of having a fixed rate is that the homeowner knows exactly when the interest and principal payments will be for the length of the loan. This allows the homeowner to budget easier because they know that the interest rate will never change for the duration of the loan.

One Year ARMs -A mortgage loan in which the interest rate changes based on a specific schedule after a "fixed period" at the beginning of the loan, is called an adjustable rate mortgage or ARM. This type of loan is considered to be riskier because the payment can change significantly. In exchange for the risk associated with an ARM, the homeowner is rewarded with an interest rate lower than that of a 30 year fixed rate. When the homeowner acquires a one year adjustable rate mortgage, what they have is a 30 year loan in which the rates change every year on the anniversary of the loan.

Balloon Mortgages - Balloon mortgages last for a much shorter term and work a lot like a fixed-rate mortgage. The monthly payments are lower because of a large balloon payment at the end of the loan. The reason why the payments are lower is because it is primarily interest that is being paid monthly. Balloon mortgages are great for responsible borrowers with the intentions of selling the home before the due date of the balloon payment. However, homeowners can run into big trouble if they cannot afford the balloon payment, especially if they are required to refinance the balloon payment through the lender of the original loan.

VA Home Loan- A mortgage loan program established by the United States Department of Veterans Affairs to help veterans and their families obtain home financing. The Department of Veterans Affairs does not directly originate VA loans; instead, they establish the rules for those who may qualify, dictate the terms of the mortgages offered and insure VA loans against default. VA loans offer up to 100% financing on the value of a home. To qualify for a VA loan, borrowers must present a certificate of eligibility, which establishes their record of military service, to the lender. VA loans, FHA loans and other loans insured by departments of the United States government are securitized by the Government National Mortgage Association (Ginnie Mae). These securities carry the guarantee against default of the United States government

Amortization

The time value of money calculations has many applications. When it comes to purchasing a home there are many applications of the time value of money procedure that can be utilized. **Amortization** is the systematic process of paying the principal along with interest as stated in a contract. In real estate the most common type of loan is an amortized loan. An amortize loan involves a series of equal payments that are made up of the principal and interest. As the loan term progresses more of the payment is applied to the principal amount. The schedule of loan payments are easily shown on an amortization schedule (Table 11.1), computer program or financial calculator. The terms of the loan depicted on the loan amortization schedule in Table 11.1 is $15,000.00 borrowed for a 1-year term with monthly payments at a 5 percent interest rate. You notice that the payment is equal through the term of the loan. You also notice that the amount applied to the principal increased each month.

Table 11.1 Amortization Schedule

Time Period	PMT	Principal Paid	Interest Paid	Total Interest Paid	Remaining Balance
Jan-14	$1,284.11	$1,221.61	$62.50	$62.50	$13,778.39
Feb-14	$1,284.11	$1,226.70	$57.41	$119.91	$12,551.69
Mar-14	$1,284.11	$1,231.81	$52.30	$172.21	$11,319.87
Apr-14	$1,284.11	$1,236.95	$47.17	$219.37	$10,082.93

May-14	$1,284.11	$1,242.10	$42.01	$261.39	$8,840.83
Jun-14	$1,284.11	$1,247.28	$36.84	$298.22	$7,593.55
Jul-14	$1,284.11	$1,252.47	$31.64	$329.86	$6,341.08
Aug-14	$1,284.11	$1,257.69	$26.42	$356.28	$5,083.39
Sep-14	$1,284.11	$1,262.93	$21.18	$377.47	$3,820.46
Oct-14	$1,284.11	$1,268.19	$15.92	$393.38	$2,552.26
Nov-14	$1,284.11	$1,273.48	$10.63	$404.02	$1,278.78
Dec-14	$1,284.11	$1,278.78	$5.33	$409.35	$0.00

With a financial calculator, there is a multi-step process that can be utilized to find the balance, principal and interest payments as any point in time during the amortization process. To demonstrate the methods used consider the flowing problem. Avis borrows $180,000 from a bank at 5% interest for a 30-year terms. Using a Texas Instruments BAII Plus we can find out how much total interest Avis pay in the first 6 years of the loan.

Table 11.2 Loan Amortization: Calculation Method

Table 11.2 Loan Amortization: Calculation Method

Example 29 Sol. Step 1	
Value	Function
180,000	PV
30 x 12 = 360	N
5/12= 0.41667	I
966.28	CPT PMT

Example 29 Step 2	
Value	Function
None	2ND
None	PV/Amort
1	P1
72	P2

Example 29 Step 3	
Value	Function
161,883.56	Bal
18,116.44	PRN
51,455.64	INT

Example 29 utilizes the TI BAII Plus Calculator Buttons, presented in table 11.2.

Step 1: Find the payment amount and keep this amount on the calculator display.
Step 2: Press the [2nd] key and [PV] key to enter the Amortization function. Under P1 enter 1 to demote month 1 or the term. Use the down arrow key to enter 72 under P2, denoting the 72nd month.
Step 3: Use the down arrow to display the remaining balance, the toil principal and total interest paid from month 1 through month 72.

UNCONVENTIONAL METHODS

There are also many unconventional methods for financing; most center around utilizing existing funds that you may have saved/invested. The upside of utilizing your own funds is that you don't have to worry about getting declined for the loan and your credit worthiness is not called into question. If you are considering going this route, you will depend heavily on your financial advisor to avoid costly tax penalties. One creative way to leverage your own resources is by creating your own banking system. A "properly designed" life insurance policy can give you the leverage to access the insurance company's money income tax-free while using your money as collateral.

Purchasing a Car

These eight steps could save you thousands of dollars on a new car. They'll also make the process quicker and stress-free.

Step 1: Research Vehicles and Pick the Features You Want

I am sure you have seen a lot of beautiful cars on the road. Whether you want gas or electric, most manufacturers have an option for you. The Internet is filled with resources to do your research; however, financing is a different issue.

Step 2: Get Pre-Approved for a Car Loan

Getting pre-approved is the best way to reduce the frustration and time that you may spend if you are not "ready" to buy. You should consider a variety of sources (i.e. bank, credit union, dealership, and self) to ensure that you properly position yourself when you find a "good deal". Having your financing on the front end allows you to be in-charge of the negotiations, since you can always walkaway if the seller's price is "not right". Once you get pre-approved, be ready to make a decision within the next 30 days to reduce the number of "hard" inquiries on your credit report.

Regardless of the financing method you choose, don't let the seller of the car you want factor that into the "price of the car". It is important to know that the "price of the car" should not be affected by the financing method. The "price of the car" is the "price of the car" and the financing method should simply enhance the deal. Don't let them play that game.

Note: The same philosophy applies to whether or not you choose to put any money down.

Step 3: Plan your Trade-In Strategy

If you don't have a trade in; skip this step. If you do, keep reading. It's important to get your trade-in value before you go to the dealership. This will help set your expectations for what the car is worth and gives you a reference point for any offers you'll receive.

The "value" of your car will differ depending on the source that you use. The Kelly Blue Book value will be different from what the dealership will offer you; which will differ from the Auto-Trader value.

There's an alternative to trading in a car or selling it yourself: The used-car retailer CarMax appraise the car and make you an offer. The offer is good for seven days, at which point you can ask the dealership to beat that price or you can sell your car to CarMax.

Regardless of how you determine your car's value, don't let the seller of the car you want factor that into the "price of the car". It is important to know that the "price of the car" should not be affected by the trade-in amount. The "price of the car" is the "price of the car" and the trade-in amount should simply lower the "price of the car" by the trade-in amount. Don't let them play that game.

Step 4: Locate and Test-Drive the Car

By now, you've settled on a few car candidates. You should see them in person before making a decision. Hundreds of dealerships throughout the country list their car inventories online, and in many cases, you can sort by color, trim level and features. This is a better way to shop than configuring a car at the automaker's website and hoping you will find one with that set of options in the real world. If you find a vehicle online, call the dealership's internet sales department to request more information. In either case, keep these do's and don'ts in mind:

- Do verify that the car you want is still in stock. It might have been sold recently, and online inventories can take a while to catch up.
- Do ask the salesperson if there are any dealer-installed options. Many new vehicles are sold with add-ons such as nitrogen in the tires, all-weather floor mats or theft protection packages. These can easily add a thousand dollars to the sale price.
- Don't just show up at the dealer on a busy weekend or late at night. Waits may be long and you may not get the salesperson's full attention.
- Do schedule an appointment for a test-drive. Early in the week and in the morning are good times. Having an appointment means the car will be waiting for you when you arrive.
- Don't just drive around the block. Take the time to see how you and your family fit in the car and see how it handles on a variety of roads.

- Do ask yourself the following questions: Are the controls easy to use? Is there enough cargo space? Will a child seat fit? (Bring it with you and test it.)
- Don't feel obligated to buy the car the same day. Feel free to take a night to think it over.

Step 5: Get a Sale Price and Ask About Extended Warranties

Once you have a target car, it's time to focus on getting a price. We recommend using one of these two ways to get a price quote on a car:
1: Call, text or email the internet sales department of three dealerships that have the car you want. Ask each for the total selling price, including any additional accessories that may have already been installed on the car. The best price will be obvious. You also can take that quote and ask the other dealerships to beat it. If you plan on leasing, this is the way to go.
2: Make sure you ask the salesperson to email or text you a breakdown of the "out-the-door price," with all the taxes and fees factored in. That lets you see the total amount you'll be spending.

You also should ask for a preview of products the dealership plans to offer you after you buy a car — things like paint protection, an extended warranty and possibly a pre-paid maintenance plan. Usually, you won't hear about these until much later in the shopping process, but we suggest you get some information now to relieve pressure later.

Here's how you do it: Call the dealership finance manager and ask about these products and services. They may be of value to you, but just know that the price is often negotiable and you don't have to buy them when you buy the car, unless you intended to fold their price into the purchase contract.

Step 6: Review the Deal and Check for Dealer Financing

Now that you have a price quote for the car, your big question is probably whether it's competitive. It's important to keep in mind that an average price paid is exactly that. Some people have paid more and others paid less. Some shoppers are only happy if they grind their way to a rock-bottom price. But for most shoppers, that usually isn't worth the hassle and frustration. If your price quote is above the average, it's not necessarily a reason to walk away from a deal.

Here's why:

A car's price isn't the only factor that determines a good car deal; however, the financing, down payment, nor trade-in should be part of that consideration. There are some intangibles, such as how the salesperson and the dealership treat you, and the time you save in the shopping process. Those are all factors in a good deal. In fact, at this point in the process, you may be able to improve parts of it.

In Step Two, you got pre-approved for financing. Now that you're close to purchase, there's a chance that you can get a better interest rate at the dealership.

To see if that's possible, let the dealership run a credit report and assess your interest rate. Or, if you know your credit score, tell the finance manager what it is and the rate for which you'd qualify. You can give your information to the finance manager over the phone. Some dealerships have credit applications on their websites and you can fill one out. If the interest rate is lower than the one in your pre-approved loan, go for it. If not, you already have a good loan locked in.

Step 7: Close the Deal

If the price, financing and fees look right, it's time to say "yes" to the deal. From here, you can proceed in one of two ways: buy at the dealership or have the car and paperwork delivered to your home. Most people tend to wrap up the sale at the dealership. Once you've agreed on a price, the salesperson will take you to the finance and insurance office. Here, you'll sign the contract and purchase any of the additional products we discussed earlier, such as an extended warranty. The alternative is to make the sale contingent on having your new car delivered to your home or office. This is a great time saver and allows you to close the deal in a relaxed environment. Regardless of where you finalize the deal, review the contract carefully and make sure the numbers match the out-the-door breakdown. Be sure there are no additional charges or fees. A good finance manager will explain each form and what it means. Don't hurry. Buying a car is a serious commitment. And remember: There is no cooling-off period. Once you sign the contract, the car is yours.

Step 8: Take Delivery

Whether you take delivery of your car at the dealership or at your home, it should be clean. The gas tank should be full. Give the car a final walk around, checking for any dents or scratches that might have occurred during transport. Finally, let the salesperson give you a tour of your new car. This includes showing you how to pair your smartphone via Bluetooth and demonstrating other important features and safety devices. All this is in the owner's manual, but let's face it, very few people ever read that book, which can be hundreds of pages long. If you don't have time for a complete demonstration when you sign the contract, set up an appointment a week or so later. With the amount of technology that comes in most new cars, that walkthrough is important and very useful. You'll learn tricks and shortcuts you might not find on your own.

Renting a Car

When it comes to documentation, each car rental agency has a policy that may differ from other companies. Before booking your car rental, call or email the rental agency and request a list of required documents in writing. Many car rental agencies charge hidden fees for secondary drivers, out-of-state trips, mileage overages, or a myriad of other state or government surcharges. Check the bottom line before you sign. There are a few required documents that must be presented when renting a car. These documents include, a valid driver's license, an active credit card and car insurance.

Driver's License: A state-issued driver's license is required to rent a car in the United States. Not only does a license ensure that you are a legal driver, but it doubles as proof of age. It is commonly assumed that you have to be at least 25 years old to rent a car, but this is not the case. In the U.S., the minimum car rental age is 21. Drivers aged 21 to 24 will